WRITE YOUR WAY OUT OF DEPRESSION: PRACTICAL SELF-THERAPY FOR CREATIVE WRITERS

Rayne Hall

Alexander Draghici

WRITE YOUR WAY OUT OF DEPRESSION: PRACTICAL SELF-THERAPY FOR CREATIVE WRITERS

Text by Rayne Hall and Alexander Draghici

Book cover by Erica Syverson and Uros Jovanovic

© 2016 Rayne Hall

November 2016 Edition

ISBN-13: 978-1539969600

ISBN-10: 1539969606

This book is not intended as a substitute for professional medical advice. If in doubt, consult your doctor.

British English.

CONTENTS

RAYNE'S INTRODUCTION

Dear Reader,

Do you feel like you're trapped in a dark hole of morass, sinking deeper and deeper, the mud rising to your hips, your chest, your throat? Is despair smothering you like a heavy blanket? Is your own life moving past you like a train, and you are forced to watch and cannot board? Has crippling lethargy wrapped its tentacles around you so tightly that you cannot move, sucking from you all energy and the will to live?

If you want to get better, to feel alive again, if you want to step out of this darkness and take control of your recovery, this book can help.

I've been there. I understand.

I've slashed my arms—with scissors, with seashells, with broken glass, with anything sharp I could lay my hands on—to get relief from the rage of knives tearing inside me. I've had days when I could not summon the energy to get out of bed, suffered waking nightmares of gruesome realism, and had panic attacks when my heart pounded so fast I knew that my chest would not stand it and would burst. I've sat on the edge of the suicide cliff at Beachy Head, my legs dangling over the abyss, ready to push myself off into the bliss of oblivion.

After years of medication, of therapy, of living in care homes for the mentally ill, of being certified as a 'mentally disabled person' I've learnt more about this monstrous illness than I ever wanted to know.

My experience is not exactly the same as yours—what you are going through is unique—but you can trust me that I won't fob you off with platitudes. I'll take your suffering seriously. I'll believe what you say you're going through. I won't tell you to 'snap out of it', because I know that if there was an easy fix, you would have done it.

People may tell you that 'it's all in your mind'. They are right, but not in the way they think. Your brain is the operating system of your body, of your psyche, of who you are. And this operating system is running amok, sabotaging itself. A malfunctioning brain is the scariest illness of them all.

When I look back at those years of darkness and the many strategies I tried to break free, I can see how some methods worked and others failed. What worked best, what ultimately helped me become alive again, was writing. I used writing—specific practical exercises, some assigned by a therapist, some I discovered myself—as a therapy.

If you're a writer, you can take this path too. Your skill with words, your fiction writing experience, your ability to rephrase statements have the power to change your thoughts, and with it your feelings. You can even re-programme your operating system, the brain.

In this guide, I'll teach you my fourteen most effective strategies. Treat them as assignments which you can do in any order. Pick the ones you want to do—the ones which inspire you, or simply the ones you have the courage and energy for. You can set your own pace, decide how often you want to work, for how long and at what intensity. You are in charge.

You may want to get a journal for these exercises. There's something inspiring about opening a brand new notebook to write in, do you find that too? I like writing in inexpensive, ruled hardbacks, preferably with coloured gel pens.

The assignments can make you feel better, and in some cases, you'll feel an immediate improvement as soon as you've completed one. They can help you overcome depression in the long term.

However, full recovery is a long journey, and you'll need to work towards this goal, which can be difficult if you're hampered by depression symptoms such as a lack of motivation, weak willpower and an inability to concentrate. Depending on how deep in the pits you're stuck, you'll probably need other support as well. This book can help you, but don't expect miracles.

I'm not a psychologist (though I hold a Master's degree in Creative Writing & Personal Development). I'm simply a writer and depression-survivor, like you. For a professional perspective, psychologist Alexander Draghici will expand on my strategies with expert advice.

This is a practical book, based on solid science but uncluttered by technical jargon and academic references. It's all about you: your feelings, your way with words, your ability to heal yourself.

Are you ready to join me on this journey?

Rayne Hall

ALEXANDER'S INTRODUCTION

Dear Reader,

There's a story I usually tell my clients who are struggling to understand where depression came from. A story about our ancestors and how for them, depression was actually a 'guardian angel' that kept them out of harm's way.

During those days, the world was a dangerous place even for the strongest and smartest of our kind. Hundreds of fierce predators waiting in the shadows, tribes fighting for supremacy, harsh weather conditions, incurable diseases and of course the ever-present chance of being mugged or killed by your own neighbours. Occasionally, even the strong or the wise were forced to experience the bitter taste of defeat which often left them weak or wounded. How did they survive to fight another day? Well, they survived because their brain told them to retreat and regroup; to seek solitude in some hidden cave where they could lick their wounds without being disturbed by predators.

Do you see the similarity between this story and your story? Just like your distant ancestor who would retreat after a serious defeat, you have separated yourself from society and chosen solitude after a terrible event (or set of events). The only reason why depression still exists in our genetic code is that at some point in our evolutionary past, this strategy was actually a reliable defence mechanism. The more you contemplate this explanation, the more you'll see that depression is a relatively normal response that becomes dysfunctional in the context of our contemporary society.

As a specialist, I guarantee that there are many definitions for depression but none of them are truly helpful for someone who's struggling with this unpleasant condition on a daily basis. This is the reason why, whether it's depression, anxiety or any other issue, I always encourage my clients to find their own definition; a simple phrase that has meaning in their specific context.

The reason for this approach is that depression and all other mood disorders can come in many 'shapes and sizes', depending on each person's unique traits. If depression is shaped by your own personality and character traits, it's fair to assume that the most effective intervention would be one designed for your specific needs.

Most of the strategies you'll find in this book are actually derived from techniques and approaches therapists often use with their clients. The only difference is that our strategies make good use of one skill you can practise—writing. Throughout this journey, you will explore your painful past, make peace with your inner demons, regain control over your thoughts and emotions, restore your sense of freedom and autonomy, plan a brighter future, and also prevent depression from ever interfering with your life.

Regardless of how depression manifests from one person to another, one thing's for sure, there's always a way to overcome it. Even the fact that you're reading this book, despite your lack of energy and despite the stubbornness which keeps you in the comfort zone, puts you on the right path towards healing. Some strategies may seem dull, others might spark your interest, and you may even find one that seems impossible to perform. Regardless of your preferences, the best course of action would be to try each of our techniques to see which work best for you.

In my career, I was surprised to see people who managed to escape depression just by getting involved in a meaningful activity (a job, a new hobby, etc.) and sad to see people who, despite therapy, medication and countless interventions, couldn't get rid of this problem.

The point I'm trying to make here is that depression and mood disorders in general are complex phenomena that can't be overcome just by swallowing a pill or using a specific technique. There are no absolute guarantees, 'bulletproof' treatment plans or infallible techniques; only probabilities, chances and your willingness to try various techniques until you find the right one.

A certain strategy may work miracles in eight out of ten cases, but what happens to the other two? Sometimes, even the most experienced mental health professionals can be baffled by their client's spectacular progress, or disappointed by the ineffectiveness of a generally accepted technique.

But just because we don't have a hundred per cent effective strategy against depression doesn't mean all hope is lost. The key is to keep trying until we find that one (or several) technique which seems to work well for us.

What I've discovered in my experience is that the process of searching for a suitable technique can often take a person's mind off those troubling thoughts and painful emotions. Maybe the best approach to depression is not a specific technique, but our perseverance and the willingness to keep on fighting against all odds.

Advice from a mental health professional can shed some light on your journey, and help you measure the risks and gains of your struggle against depression.

Alexander Draghici

RAYNE'S STRATEGY 1: GRATITUDE LISTS

In your journal, write a list of twenty things you're grateful for. I suggest you start by writing today's date (it's always good to date every entry, so you can record your progress), and then number the lines from 1 to 20.

Start every line with 'Thank you for...'

Your entries may look like this:

1. Thank you for the coffee.

2. Thank you that the rain has stopped.

3. Thank you for the great thriller I'm reading.

4. Thank you that the train is running on time.

5. Thank you for the pretty new scarf.

6. Thank you for my darling cat.

7. Thank you for Emily's phone call.

8. Thank you for a good night's sleep.

And so on.

If your depression is severe, this assignment can be challenging. Your depressed brain may struggle to come up with any positives. It may tell you that there's nothing in your life to be grateful for, and that even the few things which are good aren't the way they should be.

Even when you manage to find something to be grateful for ("I have a roof over my head. I have two healthy legs") your depression-programmed mind will immediately produce a 'but' disclaimer;

"But the rent is higher than I can afford." "But the arthritis in my hip is getting worse."

That's normal. Depression has 'programmed' your brain to produce negative thoughts by default. You have to override this default.

Don't fight those negative thoughts... simply ignore them. Write down only the good things you're grateful for.

This trains your brain to focus on the positive. Your brain is like a muscle—the more you challenge it, the stronger it grows. In this case, you're training the positive thinking muscle, which really needs all the strength you can give it.

The more positive thoughts you manage, the better you will feel. And the more you practise, the easier it gets.

This exercise has another welcome effect. Have you heard of the phenomenon that what we think about most, we attract into our lives? This effect is sometimes referred to as 'manifesting' or 'law of attraction', and many books and theories have been written about it. What matters right now is not **how** it works, but **that** it works.

The problem is, while you're in the grip of depression, your mind produces one negative thought after another, focusing on your worries, frustrations, fears and hurts. This calls more and more of the bad stuff into your life—and you really have more than enough of that already!

By focusing on what you're grateful for, you're filling your mind at least partially with good thoughts, and this will attract the good things that you sorely need.

Try to fill all twenty lines. If it's difficult at first, persevere. Each time you do this exercise, it will get easier. However, if you really can't come up with enough items, just do what you can. A little is better than nothing.

Each time you do this exercise, think of new things or repeat the ones you've used before if they still apply.

Are you religious? Address your thanks as a prayer to God (or Goddess, Allah, Krishna, or whatever name you use for the divine). "Thank you, God, for..."

I suggest you do this exercise every day. Soon after waking up in the morning is ideal, because the first thoughts and feelings set the mood for the rest of the day. Give your days a good start.

You can also do it in the evening. The subconscious mind processes during the night what you've thought about during the day, and it pays most attention to the thoughts of the hour before sleep. If you think about gratitude during that time, your brain will process gratitude during the night hours, which means your positive-thinking muscle gets a strengthening workout while you sleep.

FROM MY PERSONAL EXPERIENCE

In the early stages, I felt so bad about everything, I struggled to come up with five good things, let alone twenty.

In the grip of severe depression, I could not think anything positive without it immediately turning into a negative.

I thought "I have enough food to eat"—but even before I'd written this line down, my brain changed it to "I'm too fat."

As soon as I thought "My flat is warm and cosy" my brain told me "This month's heating bill will be enormous."

But it got easier and easier.

And something remarkable happened: each time after doing the exercise, I felt better than before I started.

Even better: after a week of doing this daily assignment, more good things came into my life. Was this coincidence? I think not.

I still do this exercise every day, and it's become a pleasant routine. Now my pen flies easily across the page, filling the twenty lines without hesitation. Most days I can't stop at twenty, because so many blessings have come into my life and my heart brims with gratitude.

ALEXANDER'S EXPERT ADVICE

Out of all the positive emotions that your mind can generate, nothing works better against depression and negative thinking than gratitude.

Just to make things clear right from the start, being in a state of gratitude towards yourself, others or the world in general doesn't mean that you deny the existence of everything that's bad or ugly. On the contrary, you accept the negative (and less pleasant) side of things and consciously choose to ignore it while shifting your attention towards the good things that have happened to you.

It's true that depression often feels like a dark shadow, clouding everything that's good and beautiful in your life, but let's not forget that we're talking about **your** inner universe; **your** subjective reality. The objective reality that exists out there hasn't changed a bit, which means you can still find plenty of positives to be grateful for.

Gratitude is like a bandage covering the painful wounds of depression; it's like an ointment slowly healing the bruises that depression has inflicted on your psyche for far too many years.

Slowly but surely, by keeping a list of all the things you're grateful for and filling it on a daily basis, gratitude will become an internalised process, a habit that feels so natural and authentic you won't need a pen and paper to practise it.

But before you get to that point, make sure you fill your gratitude list each and every morning. Maybe you won't be able to fill twenty lines right from the start; maybe even ten lines are difficult to fill and that's perfectly OK. As long as you make an effort to write at least a few things you're grateful for, you can count it as a victory.

RAYNE'S STRATEGY 2:
DESCRIBE YOUR EMOTIONS

While you suffer depression, your brain produces intense negative emotions: grief, anger, resentment, fear, inner pain, regret, shame, guilt, worry, envy, self-loathing and more.

As a writer, you have a powerful tool to reduce these emotions: simply use your descriptive skills. The effect is astonishing and fast.

Here's how you do it:

Whenever you feel bad, identify the emotion. Observe where in the body you feel it, and how it feels.

Describe it. Use a simile (a comparison with something else).

- "I experience… It feels like..."

- "I experience… It feels as if..."

Here are some examples from my own notes:

- "I experience fear. It feels like a giant iron fist clutched around my chest, squeezing the air from my lungs."

- "I experience anger. It feels like hot acid rising from my stomach into my throat."

- "I experience worry. It feels as if I had an ugly toad squatting between my shoulder blades."

- "I experience inner pain. It feels like a knife ripping inside my gut."

By labelling and observing your emotions, you're objectifying them. They lose their power over you.

At the same time, you're becoming a better writer. You're creating vivid emotional descriptions which you can use in your fiction. In years to come, whenever a point-of-view character experiences one of these emotions, you can look up your notes about how it felt to you. You'll have a fresh, original description that will dazzle your readers with its raw, vibrant authenticity.

Don't worry if you can't come up with brilliant prose. Just describe what you feel.

FROM MY PERSONAL EXPERIENCE

I discovered this technique after a session with a cognitive-behavioural therapist who advised me to label and observe emotions so I would recognise them.

This was tremendously helpful—and I immediately saw that this therapy could double up as practical writing research.

It got to the point where I actually welcomed the negative emotions: ("Ah, jealousy! Great, that's a new one for my collection.") I felt pleased about the bad feeling… and that immediately gave me a boost.

Those phrases have been so useful in my fiction writing. If you read my short stories and novels, you'll come across sentences like these:

- "The iron fear of fist clutched around his chest and squeezed the air from his lungs."

- "Anger rose like hot acid from her stomach."

- "Worry squatted like an ugly toad between her shoulder blades."

- "Pain ripped like a knife in his gut."

Book reviewers often praise my skill at conveying emotions in a fresh, vivid way. One reviewer even quoted the sentence about the ugly toad as an example of my original writing.

ALEXANDER'S EXPERT ADVICE

For a person who struggles with depression, getting a handle on those negative emotions can sometimes feel like a herculean task. Depression is often perceived as a deep and heavy fog which clouds your judgment and prevents you from finding your way out. You feel 'bad', but you don't know how to describe your emotion and this will most likely cancel your ability to exercise control over your feelings.

By using writing as a therapeutic tool, you'll be amazed to see how your once hazy emotions will slowly begin to take shape right in front of your eyes. In other words, you're no longer fighting in the shadows but on an open field.

Think of it this way, people who struggle with depression tend to ruminate a lot. They spend hours thinking about various causes, factors and consequences of their negative mood. The main problem with rumination is that it leads nowhere. You're like a lost explorer, going in circles, thinking that this path or the next one might get him out of trouble. Writing down your thoughts and emotions is the equivalent of climbing atop a tree in order to get a better sense of direction. More specifically, it gives you the opportunity to temporarily separate yourself from that confusing mix of negative thoughts and emotions, and become an outside observer who can clearly see the big picture.

Metaphorically speaking, the act of putting your emotions on paper symbolises your attempt to externalise them. Even more, by describing each and every one of your troubling feelings, you make an effort to understand the very core of depression, thus taking the first steps towards healing.

Just like the profiler who manages to sketch accurate portraits based on vague descriptions, you too can create a detailed image of your negative emotions just by putting a few words on a piece of paper. In fact, you can even improve this exercise by painting/drawing a picture for every emotion that you've described.

RAYNE'S STRATEGY 3:
PAINT BEAUTIFUL WORD PICTURES

This is an exercise for whenever you're away from home.

Write a vivid description of the place—but only of the beautiful things. Look around and listen for anything pleasing, and write it down.

Let's say you're sitting on a bench by the seaside. Describe how the sea surface glints like diamonds on crinkled silk, how gracefully the seagulls glide overhead, how exuberantly the dogs bound and play in the water, and how the waves rustle softly across the pebbles.

No doubt your depression-programmed brain will point out plenty of ugly and irritating things: dog turds fouling the beach, carelessly dropped litter, a mother yelling at the baby in its pram, a stink of dead fish and petrol fumes. Simply don't write those down.

This is another exercise in focusing your brain on the positive, strengthening that positive thinking muscle.

You'll also focus your mind on the present experience, which is useful if you're prone to worrying about the future or ruminating about the past.

At the same time, you'll gain descriptions of all kinds of places. In the future, when you need a description of a beach, a laundrette or the inside of a railway carriage, you can look up your notes and adapt them to suit your story.

If you do this exercise once a week, you'll have 52 descriptions at the end of the year, and if you do it daily, 365. That's 365 different places, described in your unique voice. (Don't worry if your descriptions lack literary brilliance. They are just notes, to be shaped and polished another time.)

FROM MY PERSONAL EXPERIENCE

Seeking the positive in the present helped me get away from persistent painful thoughts about the past, which were one of my big problems.

I really treasure those descriptions and use them a lot in my fiction writing.

However, I wish I'd picked more varied places. I find I have more descriptions of coffee shops than I'm likely to use in a lifetime. More notes about townscapes, vehicles and old buildings would be useful.

I also wish I had taken more care to write legibly, because my handwriting can be difficult to decipher.

ALEXANDER'S EXPERT ADVICE

Most experts (myself included) agree that depression is mainly fuelled by painful memories and regrets. Maybe you regret a certain decision that you think is the cause of your suffering, or maybe you feel guilty for not doing the things that would have prevented the painful reality you're living in.

If a thousand artists portray the same image, each in his own way depending on what his talent (writing, painting, sketching, etc.) is, no two will create identical pieces. This means it's in our power to capture reality and highlight its most pleasant or unpleasant aspects.

Since your mind has focused on the painful past for far too long, seeing the bright side of things might be difficult at first. As always, there are no magical solutions, only sheer willpower and a drop of perseverance. If you can't find the right words to describe what you see, hear, smell, taste, or touch, try enhancing your vocabulary by reading fiction or novels. Let's not forget that talented writers are avid readers.

Lingering in the past is the main reason why depression seems to grow larger and larger, slowly taking control over your entire experience and 'forcing' you to see the negative side of things. Your mind might not be used to keeping the good memories, which is why writing is the perfect solution for immortalising the beauty and goodness that exists all around you.

Painting beautiful word pictures is not just a strategy designed to help your mind focus on the positives, but also an excellent exercise for improving your writing skills. Who knows, maybe this exercise could represent the birth of your career as a writer.

At times depression is so excruciating and persistent that our mind can't perceive any beauty at all. In such cases, I recommend a 'technical' description. In other words, simply mention the observable characteristics of a certain objects or landscapes. For example, a mountain can be "a majestic rock giant rising above the clouds", or simply "a considerably tall, cone-shaped structure comprised of strong materials". It might not sound poetic, but at least it's a clean, accurate and purely objective description, free of any negative vibes.

RAYNE'S STRATEGY 4:
VENTING IN YOUR JOURNAL

When worries overwhelm you, when you're bursting with fury, when grief eats you alive, you need to vent. Bottling up thoughts and feelings makes them ferment, and that's when they become dangerous.

But understanding listeners aren't always available when you need them. Friends and family may not be in the mood. Some may even tell you to quit whining. Trusting people with your innermost concerns poses a risk. They may label you crazy, mock you, reveal your secret to someone else, try to manipulate you for their own agenda, or years later turn the confidences you shared against you.

Some things you may not want to share—perhaps because you're not ready, because you need to protect others, because society would consider you in the wrong for feeling that way, or simply because it's not anybody's business. You may not want anyone to know that you hate your mother, or that you spent your teens as a sex slave to your brothers and their friends.

Professional counselling is great if you can get it, but appointments need to be scheduled in advance, often involve waiting lists, and cost money you may not be able to afford.

Journaling is the perfect solution. Write about what bothers you. The moment you put it down on paper, the painful pressure inside you will ease. Journaling won't make the pain go away, but it takes the edge off it.

The trick is to write fast. Just write, write, write without pause, whatever comes to mind. Don't try to create beautiful prose, just get it off your chest. Don't censor your thoughts, don't edit them. Don't even analyse the issue.

If you pause to think, you reduce the power of the vent. Overthinking can sabotage the honesty. It can also lead to rumination (dwelling on the issue) which can reopen wounds and renew the pain—not an effect you want.

So write fast, let it pour on the page, don't judge, don't edit, don't ruminate.

You can do this exercise regularly—perhaps once a day—or simply whenever you feel the need. Tell your journal what frightens, worries, angers you now, as well as the dark secrets you never told anyone.

Find a safe place to keep your journal. You need to be sure it's safe from your parents', spouse's, kids' and flatmates' prying eyes.

VARIATION

You can also use your journal for slow, reflective writing, analysing what went wrong and gathering ideas what to do about it. This is different from speed-venting, but also incredibly helpful.

Be careful: there's a thin line between reflecting and ruminating. In simple terms: if it leaves you feeling energised and leads to solutions, it's constructive, so keep doing it. If it leaves you feeling dejected and leads to pain, it's destructive, so stop.

FROM MY PERSONAL EXPERIENCE

I found journaling extremely helpful, even at the very early stages of my recovery. I experimented with different methods, such as writing daily letters to myself and sealing them in coloured envelopes, and typing on the computer with journaling software. What worked best was writing in a ruled hardback notebook (which was small enough to carry with me everywhere), using coloured gel pens (the colours added an element of fun), on the right-hand pages only (leaving the left-hand pages for adding comments later).

For several months, I fell into the trap of rumination and stayed stuck there. Instead of just venting, I analysed, speculated, relived events over and over, wallowed in regrets. My thoughts kept going round and round, boring deeper, like a screw drilling into wood. Instead of loosening, the pain gained a firmer hold.

When I stopped ruminating (on a therapist's advice) and instead focused on simply venting, I felt much better.

Once I was well into recovery, I took up reflective journaling again, but this time without rumination.

ALEXANDER'S EXPERT ADVICE

Solution-centred approaches such as cognitive-behavioural therapy (CBT) or rational emotive behavioural therapy (REBT) are huge advocates of the thought journal. Since most of our emotional issues are the result of dysfunctional, negative thoughts that keep buzzing inside our head, we could argue that a journal may actually be one of the most powerful weapons against depression.

Besides the obvious cathartic effect that a journal has on our troubling emotions, there are plenty of other advantages that result from putting your thoughts and feelings on paper.

First, the journal is an extension of your mind; a safe space where you can store all sorts of thoughts, memories, ideas and feelings, without having to worry about stigma, ridicule or destructive criticism.

Second, the journal can be used as a 'lab' or workroom; a place where you can meticulously 'dissect' your thoughts and reveal their irrational core. But as we mentioned at the beginning of this chapter, there's a fine line between reflecting and ruminating. If keeping a journal is something new to you, perhaps it would be wiser to use it exclusively for venting.

Third, keeping a journal improves your expressive writing. Considering that thoughts and emotions are abstract concepts, sometimes (especially when you're under the unbearable weight of depression) it can be quite difficult to find the perfect words to describe your mental state. By putting your thoughts and emotions on paper on a daily basis, your writing skills will gain a certain fluency which also translates into mental fluency, since language is both an internal and external process.

Last but not least, journaling often sparks creativity. When you deny censorship and allow your inner universe to freely unfold right in front of your eyes, amazing things can happen. For instance, you may come up with insights about yourself and your issues or even explore solutions that have never crossed your mind before.

RAYNE'S STRATEGY 5:
LINE-EDIT YOUR THOUGHTS

The technique I'm going to show you uses your skill with words. 'Normal' people may find it difficult to grasp this concept, let alone to put it into practice, but as a writer, you'll be in your element.

What you think creates and shapes your feelings—and I'm sure you want to change how you feel, because having those awful emotions all the time sucks.

We've already done some 'content editing' of your thoughts in the previous chapters, especially with the gratitude lists.

Now we're moving on to 'line editing', those small stylistic tweaks where you change a word here, alter a sentence structure there, to ensure you get exactly the effect you want.

You've probably done this many times on paper or the computer, whenever you revised your own stories, edited a client's manuscript, or swapped critiques with writer friends. You know how to do it. The only challenge is doing it with thought words instead of with written ones.

STEP 1

Replace 'I am' with 'I feel' for unpleasant things.

Before:

- "I am depressed."

- "I am angry."

- "I'm confused."

- "I'm tired."

- "I am stupid."

After:

- "I feel depressed."

- "I feel angry."

- "I feel confused."

- "I feel tired."

- "I feel stupid."

In the first version, you identify with the bad stuff. You become the depression, anger, confusion, stupidity—and that's a very bad state to be in.

In the second version, you acknowledge the emotion, but you don't identify with it. This method gives the bad stuff far less power over you.

STEP 2

Phrase the thought so it's clearly about something temporary, not permanent.

For example:

- "I'm going through a phase of depression."

- "I experience a bout of anger."

- "I feel confused about this."

- "I feel tired at the moment."

- "I've just done something stupid."

If you can phrase your thought so it emphasises the temporary nature of the problem, you won't feel as bad. Also, your subconscious won't mistake it for an instruction to always feel this way.

STEP 3

Find other ways to phrase negative statements in a less negative or even positive way.

Before:

- "I should clean the bathroom."

- "I always pick the wrong men."

- "I always fall for scams."

- "I've failed again."

- "I'll never achieve this."

- "This is hopeless."

After:

- "I could clean the bathroom."

- "I haven't picked the right man yet."

- "I have a lot of experience with scams."

- "I haven't succeeded yet."

- "I wonder how I can achieve this."

- "This looks hopeless."

WHEN TO DO IT

You may want to practise this technique on paper first. Write down some of the negative thoughts you often have, and create an improved (line-edited) version of each.

Next time you have a negative thought, pause and call your inner copy-editor on the job.

If you've just thought "I'm sick of this", make an effort to think the same thought again, but in the edited version: "I'm feeling sick of this right now."

FROM MY PERSONAL EXPERIENCE

I remember the first time a therapist suggested I rephrase my thoughts. She expected to have to explain the concept and to train me how to do it—but I grasped it at once and applied it with ease.

My experience as a writer and editor really helped. All I had to do was make the shift from line-editing on paper to line-editing in my head.

You may find it fairly easy, too. But because your mental abilities are currently hampered, it can take a while to get the hang of it.

ALEXANDER'S EXPERT ADVICE

The technique described here is popularly known as reframing and it is one of the basic strategies used by therapists in dealing with emotional issues such as depression or anxiety. As we mentioned in our previous chapter, most of the emotional discomfort associated with depression is due to our biased interpretations and dysfunctional thoughts.

Thoughts influence emotions and vice versa. To get rid of depression for good you have to fight on two fronts at the same time. In other words, you have to vent your emotions and rephrase the negative thoughts that cause your distress.

When, for example, you replace "*I am angry*" with "*I'm feeling angry at this moment*", anger is no longer a defining characteristic of your personality but a simple momentary impulse that will pass sooner or later.

Another word that you should definitely eliminate from your vocabulary is 'must', especially those absolutistic "musts" such as: "*I must succeed (Otherwise I'm a complete failure)*" or "*I must be the best (Otherwise what's the point in trying)*". Try to rephrase such statements by being a bit more reasonable and tolerant towards yourself. For example, "*I must succeed*" can be replaced with "*It would be nice to succeed*". This way, you no longer set impossible standards that, if not met, will throw you into a spiral of disappointment and self-pity. At the same time, you avoid "black or white" thinking which prompts you to perceive yourself in a *positive or negative* manner. Simply put, instead of labelling yourself as *angry or calm,* you choose to describe yourself as a calm person who sometimes gets angry.

As you can see, line-editing your thoughts is mainly about finding the right balance between wanting to satisfy your desire and accepting the possibility of failure as a normal part of the process. It's about acknowledging the fact that your personality is too complex and dynamic to be defined by a momentary feeling.

RAYNE'S STRATEGY 6:
WRITE FLASH FICTION STORIES

Writing fiction is a great way to feel better, because it takes your mind off your own problems for a while as you focus on the characters' problems.

It also engages your creativity—the best feel-good recipe for a naturally creative person. Every little joy you can create for yourself is a step towards recovery. You may not be able to enjoy writing as much as you used to, and if your depression is severe, you may not be able to enjoy anything at all. Do it anyway. Bit by bit, the joy will come, perhaps like a cautious visitor at first, then as a regular guest, and finally as a permanent companion.

My main advice for writing fiction is to keep it short. Writing a novel typically takes years—and that's for authors whose mental faculties are intact. You will encounter discouragement, self-doubt, lack of motivation, impaired concentration, lethargy... all slowing your progress. Your depressed mind may view the unfinished novel as a yet another failure, and you may end up beating yourself up for not completing it. I suggest writing something short instead.

'Flash fiction' is very short stories, typically under 1,000 words. They take just a few days to write (or hours or weeks, depending on your current mental state). Each completed story will give you a sense of achievement.

HOW TO KEEP YOUR STORIES SHORT

Plan your story in advance, so it won't grow into something much bigger than you intended. Let the whole plot unfold over a single day (or even over just one hour), stick to a single location, and recruit no more than four characters to act out the story.

CHOOSING THE SUBJECT MATTER

Write about something that interests you, so it holds your attention.

You have two options, each with different therapeutic benefits:

1. Write about a character who is different from you, but experiences problems related to your own, in a different context, and perhaps make their situation worse than your own. This fresh perspective can offer surprising insights, and your fictional characters' plight can give you a feeling of solidarity. Let's say you're worried about the cold weather, the leaking roof and how to pay your heating bills. You could write a story about an Arctic explorer who tries to keep warm in his tent while the fuel is running out, or about a homeless person huddling in an improvised leaky shelter.

2. Write about something unrelated to your own problems. This will really take your mind off things for a while. For example, while you're worried about the cold weather, the leaking roof and the enormous heating bills, you could write about a botanist searching for a rare plant in the tropical rain forest, or for a camel jockey trying to win a desert race.

On days when you can't think of an idea, ask a friend to suggest a topic. Or visit a website with writing prompts, and take the first you see.

WHAT TO DO WITH YOUR FINISHED STORIES

Give your file folders creative, positive names:

- "Beautiful Stories I Have Written"

- "Drafts For Brilliant Stories"

If you have bipolar disorder, consider writing first drafts while you're in an 'up' phase, and revising during a 'down'. Several bipolar authors tell me this pattern works well for them. (I don't have bipolar disorder myself, so I can only pass on what others say.)

Invite feedback from other writers. Ask them to point out what works and what they feel you could tweak to make the story even better. In return, comment on their stories. Careful: if you feel very vulnerable, their feedback may cause you hurt, so invite critiques only when you feel up to it. Look at critical feedback as a compliment: the critics obviously like the story and think it worth improving, otherwise they wouldn't have spent time on it.

You can submit your stories for publication. Getting your work accepted and published feels great. However, be aware that far more stories get rejected than accepted. You may have to send each story out 100 times or more before it finds success, and the constant rejections may leave you feeling dejected. It may be best to postpone the marketing side and focus on just writing for now.

FROM MY PERSONAL EXPERIENCE

Although I was an experienced author, I had to learn how to keep my stories short. My impaired brain simply didn't have the energy to write novels and long stories, so I had lots of unfinished manuscripts staring at me with their reprimands.

Once I had learnt how to plot really short stories (flash fiction), I became productive and wrote story after story. Years later, when I was mentally and emotionally strong again, I pulled out those stories and revised them. I submitted them to publishers and self-published them in collections. Now those stories earn me a steady flow of royalties.

I used both options—writing about the issues that bothered me, as well as about different matters to take my mind off the problems—and they both worked well.

Unlike most depressed writers, I found that critiques didn't get me down. Far from it—they gave me an almost masochistic pleasure. I joined every online critique group that would have me, and in the process I learnt a lot and grew as a writer.

Rejections from publishers, however, were often depressing. After submitting, I had to wait for months in tense silence before a reply arrived. I clicked the emails open, my heart hammering with excitement, only to have the rejection punch me in the gut: "Thank you for submitting your story for our consideration. Unfortunately..."

In those days, many magazines still insisted on snail mail submissions with stamped addressed envelopes. Every morning, I listened eagerly for the squeal of the letterbox flap, hoping it would be followed by the fluttering whisper of an acceptance letter. Instead, there was the dreaded thud as yet another rejected manuscript dropped to the floor.

Eventually the tide turned and I got acceptances—several in the same week. Yippee, this felt good!

ALEXANDER'S EXPERT ADVICE

Just like guided imagery, flash fiction stories allow individuals to project themselves into a completely different universe where everything is possible. This exercise is particularly useful for people who struggle with depression because it gives them a chance to reshape their reality by adding a touch of hope and beauty to their seemingly uncertain future. The first step in building a better future is imagining one, and by writing down your flash fiction stories you basically 'materialise' something that only exists in your head. Suddenly, it feels like your efforts become 'real' and you're no longer in the contemplating stage of the process.

But you don't necessarily have to focus exclusively on writing positive or happy stories. Keep in mind that the main purpose here is to nurture your creativity and experience the wonderful sense of achievement that you get from completing a project (even a small one). The point is, you should choose the topic based entirely on your preferences. If you feel like writing a sad or terrifying story, write a sad or terrifying story; if you feel like writing a positive or insightful story, write a positive or insightful story.

One of the best things about writing a fiction story is that it requires the use of metaphors and other language tricks that can make your writing style smoother and more exuberant. Unlike the rational mind which operates with clear concepts and logical arguments, your unconscious mind is much more responsive to metaphors. It's much easier for you and your readers to resonate on an emotional level with the hidden message of the story. Also, a positive message packaged in the form of short fiction stories filled with catchy metaphors speaks louder than a technical or plain description.

Since we're on the topic of rational thinking, there are a few tricks you can use to gain and maintain rational control over your thoughts:

1. Question everything (even your own thoughts). Not every thought, belief or idea that your mind creates deserves to be labelled as credible or true. Put your thoughts to the test by questioning their validity and purpose. Think about your thinking!

2. Avoid 'black and white' thinking. Your life is neither the worst experience ever, nor the most beautiful thing that has ever happened. It is simply a journey of 'ups' and 'downs'.

3. Don't get stuck in limiting beliefs. I'm talking about those irrational 'what if's' or 'but's' that usually precede our statements when we discuss the possibility of achieving certain dreams or goals. *"I want to write a great book, but what if I'm not up for the task?"*

4. Embrace change and adopt a flexible perspective on yourself, others and life. This means accepting the fact that thoughts are not unchangeable constructs and human thinking is a dynamic process that's constantly recalibrating to integrate new information.

If depression likes to operate under the radar in order to avoid the rigorous control of your rational mind, perhaps you should take the fight down to the deepest layers of your mind.

RAYNE'S STRATEGY 7:
BRING A HAPPY MEMORY TO LIFE

Can you recall a time in your life when you felt happy? Perhaps it was a sorrow-free period, or an enjoyable event. Use your writing skills to recreate the experience. This will release the same good feelings.

Caution: it's best not to use a happy memory of someone or something that later caused you grief. For example, don't write about your happy honeymoon if your husband turned out to be an abusive bastard or if you're currently going through a painful divorce.

If you never had a good time in your life yet, or if your depression doesn't allow you to think of good times, simply skip this exercise for now.

Here are some writing prompts you can use if you like:

- Where were you?

- What was the weather like?

- What were you wearing?

- Do you remember colours—of garments, decorations, flowers, the sky? Describe them vividly.

- Can you remember smells? Olfaction, more than other senses, evokes memories, creates atmosphere and stimulates emotions. If you can't recall a smell, use your creativity to image a scent that would fit the scene. For example: "The sweet fragrance of roses mingled with the spicier aromas of rosemary and frying fish." "The air smelled of wood smoke and freshly mown grass."

- What sounds were there? Think of background noises such as the twittering of birds, the clattering of cutlery, or a song playing on the radio. Examples: "Children squealed in excitement, grown-ups chattered, and the band on the other side of the park struck up a bouncy march." "Drums pulsed and finger cymbals clinked."

- What other sensory impressions do you recall? How about temperature? Taste? Touch? Examples: "My toes sank into the soft sand, and the cool waves lapped at my ankles with their cool caress." "A soft breeze brushed my cheeks."

- What kind of happiness did you feel? There were probably several good emotions mingling. Try to identify them. Did you feel, for example, relieved, exhilarated, hopeful, joyful, confident, blissful, grateful, cheerful, tender, relaxed, satisfied, content, triumphant, proud, validated...?

- Describe those feelings. Where in the body did you feel them, and how did they feel? For example, "My whole body filled with whirling joy", "Relief swept over me like a wave, washing away the knots of tension from my shoulders and the heavy weight on my chest." "I wanted to leap out of my chair and dance. Although I remained properly seated, my heart was performing a giddy waltz."

You may want to write this as a nice piece of prose, the kind that could stand as a scene of a novel. Polish your writing until it sparkles. The process will give you pleasure, because your mind engages with something positive in a way you enjoy, and on top of that you'll get the satisfaction of having written something really good. You can re-read these paragraphs whenever you want a quick mood boost.

FROM MY PERSONAL EXPERIENCE

This exercise was difficult for me, and for many years I couldn't do it at all. This was in part because I hadn't experienced much happiness in my childhood, and in part because my depressed brain always insisted that any enjoyable event had a bad sequel.

For example, when I recalled my triumphal dance performance at a big show, the exhilaration of whirling across the stage, my layered skirts whirling, the sequinned costume sparkling, the music pulsing in my muscles, the waves of applause washing over me, members of the audience seeking me out to thank me for filling their hearts with pleasure, the event organisers congratulating me on my success... the spoilsport in my brain immediately squashed the joy. It reminded me of how another dancer, jealous of my popularity, carried out a backstabbing and slander campaign against me. That memory snuffed out the light and smothered me with bitterness and pain.

Now I can do the exercise easily. I can focus my attention on the bright events, and simply shut out what I don't want. Like an author who types 'The End' when the characters have achieved something great and are happy, I simply end the story there, and ignore the grumpy inner spoilsport.

I think this shows how well I have recovered from depression, and how I am once again in control of my mind.

ALEXANDER'S EXPERT ADVICE

One of the most popular misconceptions about depression is that people who struggle with this problem have zero positive memories and that their entire experience is completely immersed in sadness and despair. This misconception is merely an oversimplification of what really goes on in a depressed person's head. It's not that depression kills every moment of joy and happiness that may exist (or may have existed) in your life, it's just that it makes you indifferent towards those rare but still existent events that could put a smile on your face, even for a moment.

Since depression has probably covered your happy memories with a thick layer of sadness and apathy, digging them out may feel like an impossible task. However, it only takes one shred of information to unearth a beautiful moment that was long forgotten. In other words, this exercise should be approached in a step-by-step manner. You have to patiently extract detail after detail, until the entire memory shines bright in front of your eyes.

To make the process a bit clearer, imagine you're deconstructing a ship that was built in a bottle and putting it back together, piece by piece. If you try to force the ship out of the bottle it will break, so the disappointment that results from not being able to bring out a happy memory in one piece will only worsen your depression.

Building a detailed and vivid image of an event that has brought joy in your life long ago is a delicate process that requires patience and precision. This is the reason why the entire strategy is based on recalling as many details as possible. Not only that, but the richer and more detailed your memory is, the stronger its light will pierce through the dark veil of depression.

RAYNE'S STRATEGY 8:
WRITE HORROR STORIES

Do you suffer from anxiety, phobias, psychotic fears, scary hallucinations or terror attacks?

Perhaps you're frightened of something other people consider harmless. Maybe you can't bear the sight of long fingernails, and the sound of nails scraping on a surface sends you into a panic. Beautiful and cute things—butterflies, kittens or daffodils—may fill you with terror, especially when they get close to your face. Perhaps you're scared of clothing zips and have to wear buttoned garments because you can't breathe when encased in zippered clothes. Or maybe you get the creeps when you see a balloon, a paperclip or a clown's face.

Mentally healthy people get those weird fears too, but many depression sufferers get more of them, and they're more intense. If that's the case for you, consider yourself blessed, because you have the perfect material to write horror stories like Edgar Allan Poe and Stephen King. Stories based on weird fears often get published in anthologies.

Does the thought of a certain dangerous location make you queasy? Is there an abandoned building that makes you shudder each time you pass? Does a house in your neighbourhood ooze malevolence? Do you have to brace yourself each time you climb into your attic? Are you terrified of walking a certain path? Creepy places make atmospheric fiction settings.

By putting your fears on paper and shaping them into fiction, you're taking control of them. They no longer control you. This can bring powerful, lasting relief.

Here are four steps to mine your horror material for fiction stories:

1. Make a list of everything that frightens you. You can add to this list as you go along.

2. Write a paragraph about each item. Describe it—the colours, smells, sounds, movements.

3. Describe what kind of fear you feel for each item. Does the thought of this clog your throat, make the little hairs at the nape of your neck stand up, send shudders all over you?

4. Make each frightening thing bigger, scarier, more dangerous. What if there was an invasion of killer butterflies? What if the oranges in that bowl were malevolent demons out to get you? What kind of evil could be waiting in your garden shed? Use your imagination to exaggerate the threat.

Now you have several ideas you can develop into horror stories.

For the plot, start with the main character feeling anger or unease about the item, and avoiding it. But the item becomes gradually more menacing. Other people don't take the main character's fear seriously, and tell her to just deal with it in an obvious way. But whatever the character does, it gives the item more power, and it grows in size or multiplies.

You can end the story with the main character defeating the monster, or the monster defeating the character. You can also leave it open which of them is victorious. Or they can both die, with the character sacrificing herself to save others from the menace. Another possible ending is that the character triumphs and destroys the monster—but it has already laid a hundred eggs, and they're hatching.

Caution: writing about what frightens you can be scary. Experiencing some fear during the creative process is normal—but if it causes you more distress than you can bear, stop. Set that idea aside for another time when you feel strong enough to continue. Remember, you are in charge. You decide what to write about and when.

FROM MY PERSONAL EXPERIENCE

In the grip of depression, I suffered terrible fears. Unexpected noises, being in a room with the door closed, someone touching me—anything could set off a panic attack.

Scary hallucinations intruded into my waking life. I would suddenly see my hands getting sawn off at the wrists or my legs squashed beneath heavy machinery.

Weird phobias wrapped themselves around me like slimy tentacles: telephones, spiders, garden slugs, seagulls, buses... Even the punctuation keys on my keyboard terrified me, a serious handicap to writing. I was convinced that if I clicked the apostrophe, it would shoot a poison dart into my shoulder.

Even things that I'd always been mildly frightened of, such as fire, assumed gigantic proportions. I suffered nightmares of burning alive, and the sight of a lighted match terrified me out of my wits.

I started to write stories about these fears, and felt a strange empowerment. Suddenly I was in control. I could stop writing at any time, lock the draft into a drawer or toss it in the rubbish bin. I could change events and make the monsters follow my commands. This felt unbelievably good.

I sent those stories to publishers—and that's how I achieved my breakthrough in fiction. After years of rejection after rejection, I suddenly received acceptances. Editors of printed and digital magazines wanted to publish these stories and pay me for the privilege.

Until then, I'd never thought of myself as a horror writer. Fortunately, I had many more fears I could write about, and I produced story after story. Now my own horror story collections are bestsellers, and my individual stories have been reprinted in many anthologies.

One day I decided to be really brave and write a story about fire. I considered all that came together, and based a story on this. Two remarkable things happened: my fire phobia vanished, and that story won awards. (If you want to read this story, I've included it at the end of this book.)

ALEXANDER'S EXPERT ADVICE

Whether you are dealing with depression, anxiety, phobia or any other mood disorder, there's always one common element that seems to characterise all these issues—an overwhelming torrent of negative thoughts that disrupt your daily activities. In depression, the content of our negative thoughts is usually related to grief, sorrow and self-pity, while in the case of anxiety, our worry-filled thoughts seem to gravitate around the notion of danger. Whatever the case may be, the end result is always the same—a profoundly negative mood and high level of distress that prevent us from seeing the bright side of things.

Whenever these troubling thoughts start bubbling on the surface of our consciousness, our first instinct is to fight back. Some choose to ignore them, while others are striving to think happy thoughts in hopes of casting away the 'bad' ones. Regardless of how we choose to fight against our demons, they always emerge victorious. You can't control them; you can't run away from them; and you certainly can't hide from them.

Instead of letting your fears and terrors run around unchecked and unchallenged, why not take control and put them to good use? Not in a forceful or oppositional manner, but in a welcoming, friendly way. By trying your hand at writing horror stories, you basically invite your troubles and worries to come outside and play.

Unlike those times when your negativity manifests in an uncontrollable manner, expressing your pain and inner struggle through writing is a deliberate action. In other words, it is you who decides when, where and how your negative thoughts should manifest, not the other way around. In addition, this exercise also helps you not only to tolerate and accept your 'bad' side, but also to 'capitalise' on it. To put it in a metaphor, you will learn how to turn trash into gold.

RAYNE'S STRATEGY 9:
FICTIONALISE YOUR VILLAINS

Have nasty people harmed you by their selfish carelessness or sadistic cruelty? Use them as fiction characters.

Think of the bully who terrorised you in your teens, the teacher who refused you a place on the school sport team because she didn't like the colour of your skin, the employer who drove you to exhaustion with false promises of promotion and then sacked you, the husband who tortured you every night for his sexual pleasure.

Make these bastards work for you. Use them as fiction characters, so they are in your power and have to obey.

Remember the little details which will bring the character to life— the sound of her voice when she said those nasty things, his delighted smile when you screamed in pain. Describe their mannerisms and gestures, and use their habits and favourite phrases.

You have two options how to use these characters in your fiction. Which of them will satisfy you most?

1. Depict them as villains, 'outing' their evil on paper. This can feel especially good if you've been forced to pretend that you like them, if they are respected members of society, or if nobody believed you when you told the truth. In the story you can show freely how evil these people are.

2. Punish them. Maim, maul and murder them, lock them up in prison, make them victims of a horrendous crime. Give them the fate they deserve.

Weaving stories around the evil people has several remarkable effects.

• It gives you power where previously you were powerless. Instead of you doing their bidding, they do yours.

- Instead of days or years wasted in silent suffering, you now gain some constructive benefits from the experience.

- You can vent, letting out some of the intense anger, and expressing what you're not otherwise able to tell anyone. The stories act as a valve, releasing some painful pressure. You'll feel relief.

- You will feel less resentment. You'll still hate or detest them (as is your right), but the poison of resentment that's corroding you from inside will lessen.

Caution: don't give them (or anyone else) the chance to recognise themselves in your stories, otherwise they might try to sue you for libel. Instead of depicting them exactly as they are, use them as inspiration. Change not just the name, but the age, gender, looks, job role and so on.

FROM MY PERSONAL EXPERIENCE

Writing about the nasty people in my life—especially about the chief villain—was wonderful. At a time when I was still scarcely able to feel any good emotions, fictionalising those bastards gave me my first sense of pleasure. I experienced a faint but oh-so-welcome sense of satisfaction.

ALEXANDER'S EXPERT ADVICE

Just like the strategy described earlier (Write Horror Stories), fictionalising your villains helps you regain a sense of control over your shattered mind. Mood disorders such as depression strike at the core of our personality, leaving us drained of energy and motivation.

People who struggle with depression have the same abilities as others, but they lack the discipline, motivation and willpower to put their skills to good use. From this perspective, depression acts like a barrier preventing us from expressing our true potential or a villain whose sole purpose is to create panic and despair.

First, by fictionalising your villains you acknowledge their presence in your everyday life. You no longer run away or deny their existence, but instead you make an effort to get to know them as intimately as possible. In other words, you treat your problem with acceptance instead of ignorance, and this is one of the crucial steps towards healing. As for the villain, he or she can be played by a painful memory, an unpleasant event or even a person who might have wronged you in a certain way.

Second, the most fulfilling aspect of this strategy is that it puts the fate of your villains in your hands. You can minimise (or maximise) their impact, alter their shape, ridicule or mock them, test their strength, put them in chains, strip them of their power, and finally put them out of their misery. Whether you choose to show mercy or vengeance, the decision is entirely yours to make and this will put you in that much-desired position of power.

In addition, since you're the author, you have complete freedom to build the entire story according to your personal preferences, needs and desires. You're more than just the judge, the executioner or the brave hero who defeats his opponent (the villain). You are the architect, the creator, the one who pulls all the strings and decides the fate of his characters. In this entirely new world that slowly takes shape under your rigorous guidance, all characters (including the villains) submit to your will and your will only. In here, the villain who has terrified you for far too long is just another character that you can quickly wash away with the stroke of a pen.

RAYNE'S STRATEGY 10:
ACTIVATE DIFFERENT PARTS OF YOUR BRAIN

Vary how you write. This will give different parts of your brain a good workout and strengthen them. Like going to the gym and exercising muscles you don't use in everyday life.

You will also stimulate your creativity and may come up with solutions to plot problems and more fiction ideas than ever before.

Here are several suggestions—some easy, some challenging. Experiment with the ones you like.

- Switch between typing on a keyboard and long-handing in a notebook.

- Write with differently coloured pens, perhaps red one day and green the next, purple for the first draft and pink for the second, or use a different colour for every paragraph.

- Write on different surfaces: blank paper, ruled paper, coloured paper, crinkled paper, cardboard, old envelopes. (This method isn't suitable for working on advanced drafts, but it's great for the ideas-gathering stage.)

- Write with your non-dominant hand. If you're right-handed, use your left, and if you're left-handed, use your right. This can be difficult, so you'll probably not get much written. But it's a great exercise for boosting your creativity, with the added benefit of strengthening your willpower. (For many depression sufferers, weak willpower is a major problem, so this is a useful workout.)

- Write in a different place. If you normally write at your desk, take your laptop or your notebook to the local coffee shop or to the park. If you normally prefer quietude, try writing in a noisy place. (But don't force yourself to go to places which make you uncomfortable or scare you.)

- Turn the lights off at night and write in the dark. Obviously, this is for working on the computer, not for handwriting, and only for a short time so you don't get eye strain.

- Play music in the background, preferably music you don't normally listen to. If you like, you can select music which evokes the setting and atmosphere of your work in progress, for example, medieval instruments for your historical romance.

- Enrich the air with scents, and see how your writing goes while your brain absorbs this sensory input. Spray yourself with perfume (not the one you normally wear), light incense sticks, evaporate essential oils in your burner, or sprinkle fragrance oils liberally around your work area. Choose a fragrance you don't use habitually, to give your brain a new experience. Perhaps you can even select a scent that matches your story's setting or theme, for example, sandalwood if you're writing about India, and pine if your story takes place in Germany's Black Forest.

FROM MY PERSONAL EXPERIENCE

For me, the experience of starting a pristine new notebook—preferably a ruled hardback—always gave me a small jolt of joy, even on bad days.

My creative output works best if I long-hand early drafts and then switch to the laptop for refinement. I find handwriting with gel pens in several different colours stimulates my creativity.

Writing in coffee shops and outdoor spaces is great, but only if I have a table of the right height. I can't write at the kind of low table some coffee shops provide. Outdoors works only for handwriting, because the glare and reflection on the laptop screen make writing difficult.

Scents help—or maybe it's the ritual of preparing the essential oil burner for the writing session.

Music increases my productivity—but only if it has a medium-to-fast tempo. This was a surprising discovery. Until then, I had played slow, melancholy music which matched my mood, and that slowed me. Faster, upbeat music not only lifted my mood but made me write much faster. Lyrics and distorted rhythms distract me. I need instrumental music with a steady beat.

ALEXANDER'S EXPERT ADVICE

The keywords in this strategy are flexibility and diversity. Depression makes the world seem dull, boring and 'flat' which is why most people who struggle with it find themselves stuck in their comfort zone; a small universe comprised of only a handful of activities that are repeated over and over again, in the exact same order and with the same lack of enthusiasm.

It may sound a bit harsh but sometimes, when creativity isn't flowing naturally from within your imagination, you have to 'force' it out by pushing yourself to do things that may be out of your comfort zone.

First, handwriting is more personal than typing. You can personalise your drafts by adding your preferred colours, writing on various types of papers and working in different environments. Because of the diversity and richness that you bring to your writing style, the mind will start making new connections, thus counteracting the dullness that depression has brought in your life.

Another huge benefit of handwriting is that it keeps you focused on the task at hand. When you work on your computer, chances are you might get distracted by email notifications, software updates, and other small interruptions that can disturb your flow; not to mention the fact that your browser is only a click away, which makes it easier for you to avoid frustration and boredom, especially when you have to overcome the infamous writer's block.

Second, from a psychological standpoint, activating different parts of your brain establishes a better coordination between the left and right hemisphere and also improves mental flexibility. In addition, diversifying your writing habits also improves your short-term memory which is especially useful in writing brief stories because it helps you navigate through characters and plots more easily and without leaving anything behind.

If we want to better understand the anatomy of creative writing, we need to take a closer look at two brain structures: the frontal and parietal lobe. Both these structures are responsible for reading and writing. The frontal lobe is associated with writing, reason and personality, while the parietal lobe helps us interpret graphic symbols. By diversifying your writing habits, you exercise these two brain structures which in turn will perform better.

Writing is a complex process that requires more than a few brain areas. The best way to keep these brain structures connected and in tip-top shape is by getting plenty of diversity and stimulation.

RAYNE'S STRATEGY 11:
WRITE LETTERS TO YOUR YOUNGER SELF

For this exercise, you'll write about two characters: the child you used to be, and the grown-up person you are now.

'Normal' people often struggle to understand the concept of interacting with their younger self. Writers tend to grasp it quickly, because they are used to inviting 'characters' to play.

Choose a time when you were quite young, and confused, disturbed, unhappy, frightened or lonely. Imagine this child as you would a fiction character: What were her or his hobbies, hopes, fears, worries, favourite foods, pets, toys?

Bring to mind the painful or bewildering situation. Jot down some notes about how she feels: ashamed, distressed, abandoned, betrayed, lonely, confused...?

Now switch to your other character, your adult persona. This person is much wiser because she or he has much more life experience—and understands exactly what the child is going through.

Indeed, Adult Self is precisely the understanding, supportive grown-up friend Child Self would have needed in that difficult time.

For this assignment, I want you to create a work of fiction. Imagine that Adult Self and Child Self actually meet.

You have two options.

1. Write a letter from Adult Self to Child Self. Write it in a language a child of that age would understand. Introduce yourself. Show your understanding of the situation, show that you care, that you're rooting for the child. Help the child make sense of what is going on. Validate the child's feelings, or show a different perspective. If someone is harming the child, state that the person is bad for doing so, and that the child is right to resent and resist. ("What Uncle Peter is doing is very wrong. It's not your fault. You're right to feel hurt.") Emphasise that you're on the child's side, even if other adults don't

believe the claims. ("I'm so sorry that Mummy doesn't believe you, because I know it's true.") Give advice, and give hope.

2. Write a dialogue scene.

Imagine the two characters meeting. What would be a good setting for this scene? Choose a place where the child would be comfortable. Perhaps they eat ice cream in the park, stroke the rabbits in the hutch, or feed the ducks on the pond.

Cover the same ground as I suggested for the letter-writing assignment, but break it up so both characters talk, alternating between the two. Child Self probably has a lot of questions, because children always do. Adult Self also asks questions, because this will encourage the child to elaborate. Make sure that Adult Self doesn't berate or lecture Child Self in any way. Like in all good fiction dialogue scenes, the characters also do something while they talk, such as stroke the rabbits or eat ice cream.

When you first consider this assignment, it may strike you as futile, because Child Self can't take the advice. It's too late to change what happened.

But this exercise has the power to help heal the deep old hurts.

For many depression sufferers, emotional injuries inflicted in childhood have left ugly, painful scars, and in some cases open wounds. You can't change the past, but you can heal.

If you find this exercise beneficial, repeat it by writing letters to (or conversing) with your younger self at different ages. Start with childhood, then work up to the teenage years and early adulthood.

FROM MY PERSONAL EXPERIENCE

I was surprised how responsive my Child Self was to this. The five-year-old was surprised that anybody cared about how she felt—this was a novel experience for her.

I gained a lot of insight about the influencing factors shaping my childhood, remembered long-forgotten details, and understood what impact seemingly unimportant events had. The exercise filled me with a mellow melancholy, but at the same time it was very soothing.

ALEXANDER'S EXPERT ADVICE

Many CBT (Cognitive-Behavioural Therapy) practitioners (including me) often switch roles with their clients in order to help them build resilience and autonomy by learning how to cope with depression by themselves. In other words, by becoming the problem, you invest the client with authority and give him/her the role of healer. People who practise this technique on a regular basis slowly learn to challenge their own irrational thinking and put their depression to the test.

This is exactly what this strategy does, but instead of having a therapist to help with the process, you're going to use something which comes almost natural to you—writing. Taking the role of 'Adult Self' and addressing the 'Child Self' reaffirms your position as an expert or a survivor of depression who can now focus on helping the inner child gain a better understanding of the context in which the problem first appeared.

The content of the letter should be written in a gentle, kind and understanding tone. You don't want to bring more pain and suffering to your already troubled Child Self. In other words, you're not just an adult, but a parent, teacher, caregiver or whatever your Child Self needs you to be.

By switching between the roles of Adult Self and Child Self what you're actually doing is accessing those impulsive and seemingly uncontrollable experiences that lie beneath the surface of your conscious mind. To be more specific, you're creating a bridge between your conscious and unconscious mind; a road that allows your deeply buried childhood trauma to travel all the way up to your rational mind where it can finally face scrutiny and gain meaning.

Since you can convince your Adult Self to communicate with Child Self, maybe you can get him/her to leave a message for your Future Self as well. Write a letter to your current self, seal it in an envelope, put it somewhere safe and open it after a couple of years. This way you can track your progress, review your goals or even save a few words of encouragement for whatever lies ahead.

Healing your painful past allows you to enjoy the present and carve a better future.

RAYNE'S STRATEGY 12:
WRITE ABOUT YOUR IDEAL LIFE

For this assignment, you will indulge in daydreaming and pure wishful thinking.

Imagine what you'd like your life to be like five years from now. Fantasise about what would make you feel content, proud, satisfied.

Write this in First Person, Present Tense.

"I live in the countryside, surrounded by fields and forests. I have a warm, quiet room to myself. My grandchildren visit me every week, and we love going for long walks together. My first novel has become a bestseller and is getting stellar reviews...."

Don't hold back. Include everything that would make you feel good. In your imagination, you can treat yourself to everything you desire.

Focus on the good, and don't even mention the bad stuff. So instead of writing, "I no longer suffer this terrible crippling pain in my leg" write "I walk with pain-free ease."

If you can, include scents, flavours, sounds and other sensory impressions. "A soft breeze brushes my cheeks." "My cute cat sits on my left, purring softly while I stroke its silky fur."

This assignments has three benefits. First, it puts pleasant images in your mind, which will make you feel better (or, if you're currently deep in the pits, it will make you feel a little less awful). Second, it strengthens your brain's positive-thinking 'muscle' (like some of the previous assignments do).

The third benefit is a little weird, and you don't have to believe it, but I suggest you keep an open mind and watch what happens. What you write about in this assignment may manifest and really come into your life.

I suggest you hand-write with coloured pens in your journal, although you can also do it on your computer if you prefer.

Keep this somewhere where you can re-read it (because reading it will revive the positive images). After a few years, you may want to revisit this daydream. Who knows, some of it may already have come true.

ABOUT MY PERSONAL EXPERIENCE

At first, it was challenging. I felt guilty about wanting so many things, and stupid for indulging in such unrealistic wishful thinking. Once I dropped those inhibitions, I enjoyed the experience, and I've been repeating this assignment twice a year.

When I visit my earliest versions, the ones I felt guilty about writing down because they seemed so unrealistic, I smile. Those 'unrealistic' wishes—having a rented flat to myself, a private flower-filled garden, a black cat, living by the sea, earning a living as a writer— now strike me as perfectly realistic.

What's more, most of them have already become reality. I'm now living in a rented flat of my own, close to the sea, and I'm earning a living as a writer. As I write the draft for this chapter, I'm sitting in my garden, surrounded by the beautiful flowers I've planted, and my sweet black cat Sulu lies on the table and watches me write.

ALEXANDER'S EXPERT ADVICE

Since you've made so much progress by exploring your inner self and getting to know your depression, the time has come for you to look towards the future; a brighter future, tailored to your needs and desires.

Year after year of pain, struggle, regret and disappointment has probably left you with little to no hope in the future. Why could anyone look forward to a brighter future when the present seems grim and hopeless? But now that the present has changed for the better, maybe you should start changing your future as well.

The main purpose of this strategy is to give you a boost of optimism and hope. Little is known about the underlying mechanism of optimism, mainly because this complex process can take many forms. But what we do know is that optimism acts like an antidote, neutralising the negative emotions associated with depression. In addition, optimism is also linked to a stronger immune system and pain resilience. Like all other things, optimism should be used moderately. Too much optimism and you lose touch with reality.

Like we mentioned earlier in this chapter, your description should be detailed, appealing (to you) and written in present tense. Although your ideal life should be filled with amazing goals and extraordinary achievements, try to keep a healthy dose of modesty by adding some smaller goals that are easier to achieve. The reason for adding these light, easily-achievable goals is that when you manage to accomplish them, the story will gain potency which of course will make you more willing to follow it.

Metaphorically speaking, writing a detailed description of your ideal life helps you bring the future into the present. To put it another way, the future tends to become more 'real' and 'tangible' once you start writing it down on paper.

Even if an ideal life seems a distant dream, writing it down on paper is that first step towards turning your dreams into reality.

RAYNE'S STRATEGY 13:
WRITE A LETTER TO A FAMOUS WRITER

Many writers experience depression—far more than the average population.

Don't worry: writing doesn't cause depression. However, it seems that writing talent and susceptibility to depression are genetically linked. The greater your natural writing gift, the more likely it is that you'll experience depression.

Years ago, as part of my work for my MA degree in Creative Writing & Personal Development, I did an informal survey among the writers I knew. How many were suffering, or had suffered in the past, from depression? The results startled me: 9 in 10! That's definitely more than 'normal'.

My message in this book is that as writers we are equipped to help ourselves, more than 'other' people. Our skill with words, our power to make things happen on the page, and our ability to shape plots and characters, are the rope by which we can climb out of the dark hole.

For this assignment, I've compiled a list of writers with depression. You'll discover many great names among them—famous novelists, celebrated poets, chart-topping bestsellers. And you're one of them.

The list is incomplete, of course. Also, it's not a certified list, because some of these writers lived long ago, before depression was a diagnosed illness. I've included these writers based on the feelings they described in their journals, because of factors in their life and lifestyle such as alcoholism and suicide, and because of their friends' observations about a surfeit of melancholia.

Mary Shelley, Virginia Woolf, Leo Tolstoy, Sylvia Plath, Charles Dickens, Tennessee Williams, John Keats, JK Rowling, Robert E Howard, Charlotte Perkins Gilman, Anne Sexton, Christina Rossetti, Dante Gabriel Rossetti, Stefan Zweig, Barbara Hambly, Kurt Tucholsky, Dorothy Uhnak, Raymond Chandler, Hans Christian Andersen, Joseph Conrad, Siegfried Sassoon, Fyodor Dostoyevsky,

Ernest Hemingway, Graham Greene, James Ellroy, Henry James, TS Eliot, Samuel Johnson, Walt Whitman, Kurt Vonnegut, Mark Twain, Sidney Sheldon, Philip K Dick, Kawabata, Robert E Howard, Lucy Maud Montgomery, HP Lovecraft, Amanda Hocking, Samuel Johnson, Rachel Kelly, Gwyneth Lewis, Agatha Christie, Catherine Cookson, King Solomon.

Study the list. Take note of any names you recognise. If you like, look up these authors' biographies and bibliographies online.

Select one writer whose work you admire. You may want to read or re-read one of this author's works.

Now write a letter to this author. Write from the perspective of a fellow-writer and fellow-depressionist. Tell the writer what you admire about his or her work, from one author to another. Remember, all writers like to hear their work appreciated, especially when the praise is for specific aspects. Talk about the writer's depression (or ask about it) and your own.

If you like, repeat the assignment, writing a letter to another writer.

With this exercise, you'll create a mental association between you and the literary greats, which will give you a confidence boost and encourage you to pursue your writing ambitions. It will also reduce any feeling of hopelessness and shame you may feel because of your illness. You're not inferior because of your illness—rather you are one of the special elite.

By the way, if any family members are looking down on you because of the stigma of mental illness, you can do a bit of name-dropping and watch them adjust their attitudes.

FROM MY PERSONAL EXPERIENCE

When I first discovered how many great writers had lived with this dark companion, I felt immense relief.

Then I grew curious about how depression and writing talent are connected. That's when I did the mini-survey among the writers of my acquaintance.

I even considered making this topic my MA thesis, although in the end I decided on a different topic (rewriting ancient myths from the perspective of the villains). But my interest in the link between 'susceptibility to depression' and 'creative writing talent' is still awake, and that's why I've written this guide.

ALEXANDER'S EXPERT ADVICE

Many people would like a career as a writer. However, only a handful of people choose this path in life and there's a good reason for that. Being a writer is no easy work. You have to revise and rewrite your material over and over again until you finally reach that point where you can say *"This is it"*. But all this work and sacrifice doesn't guarantee that readers will buzz around your book, and having to face the disappointment that results from seeing your efforts thrown out the window, can easily send you down the wrong path.

Leaving aside the frustration behind creating something truly enjoyable, writers and artists in general are more prone to self-reflection and contemplation which can be both a blessing and a curse. On one hand, self-reflection and contemplation allows them to tap into their inner potential and create wonderful works of art that might be appreciated by their audience, and on the other, it can make them more vulnerable to depression and other mood disorders.

One of the main purposes of this book is to help you deal with depression, while keeping the self-reflective or contemplative tendencies that help you create wonderful things. Basically, the things that make you vulnerable to depression (self-reflection and contemplation) will be used to fight against this problem.

To some extent, this strategy is somewhat similar to the one described in our previous chapter. Unlike the letter where you symbolically addressed your Child Self, this time you're going to have a chat with your Better Self; the one who was bullied and reduced to silence by depression.

By writing a letter to a famous writer, you unconsciously identify yourself with a better version of 'you', because that famous writer embodies everything you want to become. In a sense, this strategy is a written form of guided imagery where you envision your ideal self and then try to bond with him/her so that you can be more like him/her. Keep in mind that the goal of this strategy is to put you in touch with your undiscovered potential, so try not to imitate another writer's lifestyle or choices.

RAYNE'S STRATEGY 14:
OTHER METHODS FOR YOU TO TRY

While the focus on this book is on ways to help yourself by writing, there are other steps you can take to feel better.

Many paths and methods exist to alleviate depression, and they're neither 'right' nor 'wrong'. What matters is whether they help you. Choose the ones you want to try, and observe their effect. Whether it's prayer, acupuncture, hypnosis, medication, counselling, herbalism, or white magic—if it helps you, it's good.

Here are several I found helpful. You may want to try some of them.

1. PHYSICAL EXERCISE.

A good workout can make you feel much better. This is one of the main recommendations medical professionals give to depression sufferers. I found it definitely helped me.

The problem is that physical exercise requires willpower and energy, and both are in short supply when you're in the grip of depression. You may intend to exercise, but just can't give yourself the push to get started, and if you do start, exhaustion ends the effort.

My advice is to do a little, just as much as you can. Could you do two minutes right now? Stand up and sit down again, wave your arms in the air, walk on the spot? Do it. The two minutes you do are much better than the two hours you think about doing.

I started with two minutes, which was the maximum I could manage. But the next day I achieved three minutes, then four, then five. Gradually, I built up to two hours every day. These were mostly gentle exercises such as walking and qi gong. Some days I couldn't do much, couldn't even get out of bed—and on those days, my exercise consisted of a minute's worth of wiggling my toes. In retrospect, the effort I put into exercising was the best possible investment of my limited mental energy.

Light aerobic activity, such as walking, helped me feel better after about twenty minutes. I didn't feel great—but on a scale from one to ten, exercise always improved my mood by one notch. When I was very down, feeling even one notch better meant a lot.

I also found that if I exercised a lot one week, the following week I had much more energy. This was an important discovery, because I had very little energy in those days, and every improvement was a big step.

For inner pain, I lifted weights—very heavy dumbbells, so heavy that my muscles screamed under the weight. Feeling the muscle pain, over which I had full control, distracted me from the inner pain over which I had none.

2. SUNSHINE

Many—though not all—depression sufferers find that their condition gets worse in dismal weather and during the winter season when the days are short. If this pattern applies to you, get as much sunlight as possible. Go out during the daytime—maybe for a walk which will provide your daily exercise quota at the same time, or just to sit on a bench in the park.

On dull days, switch on many lights in your room. While artificial light is less effective than natural sunshine, it still helps a bit. You can also buy 'broad spectrum' and 'daylight imitation' light bulbs. These are more expensive than ordinary bulbs, but can help greatly. Use them without lampshades to get the best effect.

Treatment lamps are available for S.A.D. (seasonal affective disorder), which is a form of depression. Whether you have S.A.D. or not, if your mood and energy levels rise and fall with the amount of light you get, one of those lamps can be a good investment.

I feel best on sunny days and spend as much time outdoors as possible. During the darkest time of my depression, I found that using a S.A.D. lamp in the morning gave me a much-needed energy boost for the day. I still use my S.A.D. lamp to help me during the dark winter months. I have it on my desk and turn it on for a couple of hours in the morning.

3. GEMSTONES

Crystals and stones have healing powers, transmitting energy when you touch them. Some people are highly receptive to gemstones, others get no effect whatsoever. It's worth finding out to which group you belong.

I've always loved touching stones, especially sun-warmed pebbles on the beach. So when I became ill with depression, I investigated the healing energies of gemstones. Several stones can ease depression: carnelian, amber, lapis lazuli, citrine, black tourmaline.

I found that carnelian was the one for me. Whenever I felt really bad, I held a cornelian tumblestone in my hand (frankly, I clutched it in my palm with desperation) and I felt strengthening energy flowing from it which my body absorbed. This effect was strongest in the early stage of my depression, when I was barely alive. Later, when I was well on the road to recovery, I no longer felt a strong effect from stones.

If you want to give gemstones a try, see if you can buy inexpensive tumblestones. You may want to go to a shop selling gemstones, and touch several to see which ones feel right. From time to time, rinse your stone under running water to cleanse it from the negative energies it has absorbed.

4. AROMATHERAPY

Inhaling essential oils is a natural way to affect your mood, and it works whether you're mentally healthy or ill. You can evaporate the oil in a 'burner', or simply add some to a bowl of hot water. Even easier, just sprinkle a bit of oil around the room. If you're a woman, you can wear a few drops on your wrist as a perfume. (Whether you can do it as a man depends on the cultural norms of your society.)

For me, sweet orange, melissa (lemonbalm), bergamot and neroli (orange blossom) oils were the most effective when I was feeling low. Lavender helped me with fears and to calm after panic attacks, and rosemary gave me energy when I was too tired to do anything.

Other oils recommended for depression include: grapefruit, lemon, basil, ylang ylang, chamomile, rose, geranium, sandalwood, jasmine, petitgrain and clary sage. Try them and see how they work for you.

5. MEDITATION

Meditating is a great way to create a feeling of inner peace and serenity, and it can be an enormous help in easing depression.

The problem is that it's almost impossible to learn meditation skills while suffering severe depression. Learning to meditate requires mastery of one's mental faculties. If you haven't meditated before, now may not be a good time to take it up, because you might feel like a failure.

However, if you have practised meditation in the past, try to revive those skills and take up the meditation habit again.

If you haven't meditated before, I suggest an alternative: guided visualisation. This is a blend of hypnotherapy and meditation. You can buy CDs or find free downloads, some of them even designed specifically for depression sufferers. Listen to an audio-recording with your eyes closed, while the speaker (usually a hypnotherapist) tells you what to imagine. You'll enter a relaxing trance-like state of mind, possibly fall asleep, and probably come out of it feeling better.

Fortunately, I had learnt meditation years before I became ill, and although I hadn't practised for a long time, I was able to take it up again. So I sat at the beach and meditated. I also used guided visualisation CDs, and found them remarkably helpful. I listened to one of them every night as I drifted off to sleep. As an additional benefit, they reduced my insomnia.

6. CONSULT A DOCTOR

It's worth getting a professional diagnosis, especially if your depression persists over a long time, or if you feel suicidal. Once you have a doctor's official diagnosis you may, depending on your country's public healthcare system or your insurance cover, be entitled to free medication, psychotherapy or time off work.

The doctor you see may not spend much time with you, and the examination may only last five minutes, but he may refer you to a specialist who'll arrange practical help.

When I got the official diagnosis, I felt relieved. Now I had proof that I had an illness and wasn't a malingerer.

The prescribed medication (of the SSRI type, designed to stop my brain destroying crucial chemicals and sabotaging itself) helped in the early, most severe phase, lessening the worst symptoms. Later, I found that I recovered better without taking tablets. However, different patients respond differently to different medication, so your experience may be different.

I was offered group therapy, but this was not right for me. I tried a few sessions but simply couldn't bear sitting in a room with other people.

I found psychotherapy extremely useful, initially for survival strategies to get through another hour or another day, then for coping strategies for dealing with the problems, and finally, for strategies for preventing a relapse.

If you opt for psychotherapy, you will find that the exercises in this book are a helpful preparation. Your therapist may show you ways to build on the exercises you've already done, tailored to your personal situation.

ALEXANDER'S EXPERT ADVICE

In the last fifty years or so, researchers from different fields such as Biology, Psychology, Neuroscience and Philosophy have come together in hopes of unravelling the mysteries of the human mind. As a result, depression is no longer seen as divine punishment or the work of hidden occult forces. Aside from discovering the underlying mechanisms, experts have also come up with effective ways of preventing and treating this mood disorder.

You might not be aware of this, but some of the techniques used today by experts who specialise in treating depression, date back centuries ago. For example, ancient philosophers and spiritual leaders were well aware of the fact that physical activity and meditation can improve one's mood; they just didn't know how to explain the underlying mechanism.

Nowadays, we know that after a thirty-minute workout, the brain releases endorphins which can easily put us in a good mood, and that meditation can change our brain waves, thus altering our mental state. What's interesting is that knowing **how** a certain technique works makes us more willing to try it. In short, don't just practise a technique, understand it!

'By the book' interventions are not a hundred per cent effective, so always keep an open mind and explore alternative techniques. However, if you want to be certain that what you're about to try won't bring more harm than good, consult a mental health professional before doing something you might regret later.

Regardless of how you choose to address your emotional issues, know that doing something is far better than doing nothing. Since you've managed to read all the way to the end of our book, it's fair to say that you're definitely contemplating the idea of getting rid of depression for good.

Never forget that depression is not some distant evil that has come to torment you, or an issue that was caused exclusively by exterior factors. Depression is merely the product of your own thinking and since it's part of your inner self, you can definitely explore it, conquer it, control it and eliminate it.

DEAR READER,

I hope you found these strategies helpful and inspiring.

I'd love it if you could post a review on Amazon or some other book site where you have an account and posting privileges. Maybe you can describe your experience with some of the exercises, and mention which you found most helpful and in what way.

Email me the link to your review, and I'll send you a free review copy (ebook) of one of my other Writer's Craft books. Let me know which one you would like: *Writing Fight Scenes, Writing Scary Scenes, The Word-Loss Diet, Writing About Magic, Writing About Villains, Writing Dark Stories, Euphonics For Writers, Writing Short Stories to Promote Your Novels, Twitter for Writers, Why Does My Book Not Sell? 20 Simple Fixes, Writing Vivid Settings, How To Train Your Cat To Promote Your Book, Writing Deep Point of View, Getting Book Reviews, Novel Revision Prompt, Writing Vivid Dialogue, Writing Vivid Characters, Writing Book Blurbs and Synopses, Writing Vivid Plots.*

My email is contact@raynehall.com. Also drop me a line if you've spotted any typos which have escaped the proofreader's eagle eyes, or want to give me private feedback or have questions.

You can also contact me on Twitter: https://twitter.com/RayneHall. Tweet me that you've read this book, and I'll probably follow you back.

If you find this book helpful, it would be great if you could spread the word about it. Maybe you know other writers who would benefit.

At the end of this book, I've included two stories I wrote during my darkest years, so you can see what can be achieved.

I'll also adding an excerpt from another Writer's Craft Guide you may find useful: *Writing Deep Point of View.* I hope you like it.

With best wishes for your journey to recovery and your writing,

Rayne Hall

ACKNOWLEDGEMENTS

I give sincere thanks to the beta readers who read the draft of this book, tried out the strategies, shared their experiences and offered valuable feedback. I promised them confidentiality, so I won't publish their names here. You know who you are.

I also offer my gratitude to the psychotherapists who helped me on my difficult journey to recovery: Mary Locke, Hugh Maxwell, Jen Popkin and Charlotte Potter.

Thanks are also due to the members of the Professional Authors Group who critiqued individual chapters.

The book cover is by Erica Syverson and Uros Jovanovic. Julia Gibbs proofread the manuscript, and Bogdan Matei formatted the book.

And finally, I say thank you to my sweet black cat Sulu who snuggled on the desk between my arms with his paw on my wrist and purred his approval as I typed.

Rayne Hall

ABOUT THE AUTHORS

RAYNE HALL

Rayne is a freelance author who writes creepy horror stories, dark epic fantasy and practical non-fiction books. Rayne Hall has published more than sixty books in several languages under several pen names with several publishers in several genres. She is the author of the bestselling Writer's Craft series with 22 titles so far, including *Writing Dark Stories, Writing About Villains, Writing Vivid Characters, Writing Deep Point of View.*

After living in Germany, China, Mongolia and Nepal, Rayne has settled on the south coast of England in a dilapidated seaside town of former Victorian grandeur. She enjoys reading, gardening and long walks along the seafront. Her black cat Sulu—adopted from the rescue shelter—likes to snuggle between her arms while she writes.

Rayne has worked as an investigative journalist, development aid worker, museum guide, apple picker, tarot reader, adult education teacher, belly dancer, magazine editor, publishing manager and more, and now writes full time.

You can find Rayne's books on Amazon: viewAuthor.at/RayneHall.

Her website with information and tips for writers is here: raynehall.com.

To find out about new releases, special offers and writing contests, subscribe to her Writer's Craft newsletter here: eepurl.com/boqJzD. Subscribers receive a free pdf workbook *Grow Your Unique Author Voice.*

ALEXANDER DRAGHICI

Alexander is a Clinical Psychologist and a licensed Cognitive-Behavioural Therapy practitioner. His work mainly focuses on strategies designed to overcome the most common mental issues—anxiety, depression and stress. Through his practice, he promotes rational thinking and emotional awareness while helping others stay focused on the present and let go of the painful past.

During his teenage years, Alexander had his fair share of anxiety. Surprisingly, this issue of his was the spark that ignited his passion for Psychology and drove him to search for the best strategies to overcome such mood disorders. Writing is another way of reaching out to those who can benefit from his experience and knowledge.

When he's not busy with his therapeutic practice or working on his books, Alexander likes to go for a jog in the Romanian forests or at least at the nearby gym. If the weather is too chilly for an outside jog, then you'll probably find him in the comfort of his home, reading a good book or playing his guitar.

STORY EXAMPLE:
SEAGULLS

I wrote this story at a time when I was frightened of everything. Even the birds outside my window seemed evil. I used Strategy 8, 'Write Horror Stories' to pen a tale inspired by my fear. The story is quite simple—but it contributed to my success as a writer. It has become my most re-printed, most anthologised work.

While the stencils dried above the dado rail, Josie squatted on the carpet, eating her first breakfast in the new studio flat.

Three seagulls stood outside the window, white-feathered and silver-winged, their eyes yellow halos around death-dark cores. Every time Josie lifted a spoonful of muesli to her mouth, their greedy stares followed her hand.

According to the *Welcome To Sussex* pamphlet, European herring gulls were an endangered species, worthy of protection. On the brochure's cover, seagulls looked so pretty: white-feathered, silver-tipped, soaring serenely in an azure sky.

In close-up reality, they were ugly, unromantic beasts, from the wrinkled flat clawed feet and the grey-pink legs to the folded wings ending in feathers like black blades. Each thumb-long beak had a hole in the upper half, some weird kind of nose she supposed, a gap through which she could see the misty sky. Then there was the red, a splash of scarlet on each beak, as if they carried fresh innards from a slaughter feast.

A sudden screech, and they dropped their pretence at peacefulness. Big beaks were pecking at her miniature roses, ripping them out and apart, tossing green fragments.

Josie stormed to the window, waving the tea towel like a weapon. Three pairs of wings unfolded, filled the window, lifted off. Screeches of outrage tailed off into the distance.

Of the pretty pink roses she had planted with so much care yesterday, only stems and shreds remained. With delicate fingers and tender words, she pressed the roots back into the soil and gave them water to settle back in.

She returned to work, sponging the next layer of stencils, delicate blooms in pink which would go well with chiffon curtains.

*

At noon, she left the stencils to dry and prepared lunch—muesli again, since she had not had time to stock her cupboard.

The gulls were back. Sharp bills pointed at the muesli on her spoon, begrudging her every bite. The one with deep grooves on its chin knocked its beak against the window. *Tap-tap, tap-tap.* More fiercely: *klacketeklacketeckacketeklack.*

The oat-flakes stuck dry in Josie's throat.

The tallest of the gulls, with head feathers standing up like a punk's haircut, tilted its head back and trumpeted a shattering scream. *Kreeeeee! Kreeeee!* The white chest vibrated with screeches which could have brought down the walls of Jericho. Josie wasn't sure if the window glass trembled, but the shudders in her spine were real.

The gull closest to her had obscene red stains on its beak, like a vampire's bloodied lips. Josie tried not to look, but she had to. Their closeness sent chills up her back, even with the transparent safety of double-glazing shielding her from predatory beaks.

If only she had curtains in place, preferably something as thick and solid as the garish seventies drapes she'd left behind in the shared London flat.

The red-billed gull unfolded its wings, increasing its size to fill the large frame, and more. Josie ducked behind two unpacked suitcases, but still their stares followed her. The studio flat, which had appeared so spacious when she had first viewed it, now closed in on her.

Living by the sea had seemed such a good idea, especially in St Leonards, where the streets hummed with history. She had pictured herself in a dress of sprigged muslin, strolling along the promenade on the arm of a Mr Darcy. A grey bombazine gown and a Mr Rochester would be good, too.

The gulls clucked like hens, trumpeted like elephants, screamed like pigs at slaughter, the noise shrilling through the window-glass and echoing in the unfurnished room. Why had they sought her out?

She scanned the houses on the other side of the road, Regency terraces with elegant wrought-iron balconies and bow windows on pale, ornamented façades. No unwanted visitors plagued those windows, although some seagulls socialised on distant roof gables and chimney pots.

Josie thought of squirting them with water from the plant mist spray, but living in cliffs, gulls were used to splashes, and of pelting them with hazelnuts from the muesli box, but they might just let the missiles drop off their feathers and gobble up the food.

Resolutely, she pulled her floaty velvet coat from a suitcase and threw it full force against the window. The big gull stepped back and dropped off the ledge, but within moments it was back.

Josie retreated to the windowless bathroom, where she emptied a jar of perfumed crystals, a farewell gift from her flatmates, into the steaming tub. Like always, the scent of lavender soothed her. During the hot soak, she was able to view the seagulls' behaviour as a mere annoyance, and her own reaction as ridiculous.

How strange that the birds homed in on her, and how strange that she was so frightened of them. After all, they were only birds, kept out by a double panel of solid glass.

But then, she'd always been frightened easily. As a child, she feared the neighbour's dogs, just because they were big and fierce looking, while young children patted them with fond trust. She could not bring herself to go near the farmer's cows, or the ugly looking turkeys in the cage. All harmless animals, of course, and only a stupid child would be afraid of them. The other kids made fun of Josie's fears, teasing her without mercy until she despised herself.

She covered her legs in thick soapy foam and shaved them with deliberate slow strokes, a reassuring routine, and stayed in the bath until she had used up all the boiler's hot water.

By the time she had rubbed her skin dry, the gulls had departed, probably to the beach to snatch snacks from unsuspecting tourists. In the bright sun, the glass showed zigzagging white lines where beaks dribbled, and white faeces gleamed on the windowsill ledge.

With the monsters gone, she browsed the mail order catalogue for curtains and furniture, designing light-filled, romantic space with swathes of chiffon and Regency prints, and pondered what to wear when she started her new job on Monday.

During supper—more muesli—the same three gulls returned. *Klacklack klackeklack.* All three, hammering against the glass. Josie recognised the grooved throat, the blood-stained beak, the punk-style feathered head.

They knocked the window by moving their heads forward and back. Even ghastlier, the small one kept the tip of its upper beak glued to the glass, and vibrated the lower one. The whole pane rattled in an angry staccato. Josie had heard that bridges collapsed when a unit of soldiers marched in synchronised steps. Would the window break under the persistent pecking?

For the first time, she wished she was still in London, in the soulless grey tower block with views of other soulless grey tower blocks, in a flat furnished with someone's hideous 1980s leftovers, with flatmates whose unwashed dishes stank up the kitchen and whose stereos thumped through the night. The flatmates would know what to do, or would at any rate drown out her fears with their loud laughter and roaring rap.

"Oh, go away, go away!" she shouted at the beasts. Without the slightest shift of a leg, blink of an eye, twitch of a wing, they sat and stared.

She grabbed a fistful of muesli. "If I give you this, will you go?"

Kreeee-kreeeeeee. Kreeee. Impatient foot-tapping, as if they knew what was in the box.

She turned the squeaking handle, tilted the window, and dropped the muesli on the sill. They snatched the crumbs as soon as they fell, three scimitar-sharp beaks devouring the raisins and oat-flakes faster than she could dip her hand back into the box. *Kreee-kreee.*

If she gave them enough to fill their stomach, they would not bother hanging around. She grabbed another fistful and pushed her hand through the gap.

Pain shot like a piercing nail through her flesh.

She pulled her hand back, slammed the window shut and twisted the lock. Dark red blood streamed from the wound, dripping thick blotches on the pristine white windowsill.

The gulls yelled in angry triumph.

Having neither antiseptic nor a first aid kit, Josie rinsed her hand under the tap and wrapped it with an embroidered handkerchief. She needed allies, someone who had experienced this kind of harassment and knew what to do. But she had not yet introduced herself to her neighbours, and the harridan in the flat below had complained about the noise of Josie dragging suitcases up the stairs.

Dusk descended, but the gulls did not retire to roost.

Klackedekackedeklcackedeklack, they hammered at the window. Josie blessed the double glazing. Even if they cracked one pane, the second would resist, wouldn't it?

Josie scanned the other buildings in the evening mist. No seagulls were attacking the mock-Georgian retirement homes, the Victorian gothics, the concrete monstrosities from the seventies. Why had they picked her?

Maybe because she was at home when most residents were out at work. Maybe the absence of net curtains had lured them with a tempting view inside. Maybe they'd tried all the other windows, and learnt that they'd not get fodder there. She cursed her weakness of giving them muesli. Now they would not go away.

A soft, prolonged scratch. And another.

One gull was scratching along the edge of the window; the other two pecked at the putty that held the glass in the wooden frame. Josie had heard that great-tits and other songbirds sometimes nibbled at window-frame putty because they loved the flavour of the linseed oil it contained. Since seagulls didn't eat putty, what was their plan? If they pecked the stuff to loosen the glass from its frame, she would be trapped in a room with three violent seagulls hacking their beaks at her. What then?

Klackedeklack.

With her pulse thumping in her throat and ears, Josie put her door on the latch, and tried the flat next to hers, and the ones above, but nobody replied. The flats on the ground and first floors were still unoccupied after refurbishment. That left the one on the floor below.

Josie knocked and waited. A toilet flushed inside. At last, the door squealed open. "You." The sharp-nosed woman, with grey hair clinging like a steel helmet to her skull, stabbed a finger at Josie. "Do you know what the time is?"

"I, ahem…I know it's late, but…"

"Nine o'clock. Nine o'clock, do you hear?" Her voice whined like a dentist's drill, shrill, painful, persistent. "A time when decent people expect to be left in peace."

"My name is Josie Miller. I've just moved into flat six." Josie held out her hand.

The woman kept one arm locked across her chest, and with the second led a cigarette to her mouth for short angry puffs. "This is a respectable house. Or it used to be, until they refurbished and let the riffraff in."

"I assure you, I'm respectable, Mrs…" When the harridan did not supply a name, Josie said, "I'm a PA secretary at Lloyds TSB Bank, and the letting agent has my references. I'm sorry to bother you, but there are herring gulls by my window."

"In case you haven't noticed, this is the coast. Gulls live here."

"I'm just wondering how to treat them. I know they're a protected species…"

"Pests, that's what they are," the woman snapped. "Vile vermin, so don't feed them. Now excuse me. It's nine o'clock, and decent people have a right to peace."

The door clicked shut.

Josie checked her watch: eight forty-five.

*

She had to build a barrier. If she had furniture, she would push it in front of the window, and if she had tools, she would nail her blanket across. She managed to stand a suitcase on the inner windowsill, balancing her rucksack on top of it, filling the gaps with her still-wet towel and her winter coat.

Unless she held her hand very still, the pain was burrowing through her flesh. Holding the sponge for stencilling would be difficult tomorrow.

At least she no longer had to see the gulls. She lay on the carpeted floor, wrapped in her blanket, fantasising about a four-poster bed hung with drapes of rose-pink satin.

Klackedeklack. Scraaatch.

She turned on her CD player to drown out the seagull sounds. *Thada-thada-doum-thad.* The steady beat gave an excuse to her racing heart.

From below came outraged banging. The neighbour disapproved of the music. Josie plugged her ears with the iPod, but for once, the audio recording of Pride and Prejudice failed to absorb her. The fear in her stomach kept rising to her chest and throat, and she lay awake for a long, long time.

*

On waking, Josie's head ached and her throat scratched with thirst. She groped for the familiar lamp switch, and found only rough carpeted floor. Ah, yes, the new flat, and St Leonards, and the new job which had come up so suddenly.

Her brain felt like it had been boil-washed and tumble-dried. She stretched her aching limbs, scrambled up and stumbled to the window to pull the curtains back and let the dawn light in. No curtains, just a suitcase. Now she remembered: Seagulls.

When she undid the knotted hankie, she found the wound already healed over, the only slight discomfort coming from the tightness of the encrusted skin.

She lifted the suitcase away from the window. Sunlight bathed the room. Outside, cool dawn changed into a golden morning, and the distant sea sparkled like diamond-sprinkled satin. Nobody had ever been killed by a wild bird. A breath of the fresh, salt-laden morning air would drive the last of the childish scares from her over-tired head.

On the other side of the road, three white-feathered, silver-winged gulls sat squatting on chimney-pots, haloed by the morning sun, a picture of romantic innocence.

Josie turned the squeaking handle and threw the window wide open.

They rose, fluttered, soared...and then they were upon her.

STORY EXAMPLE:
BURNING

I wrote this story as self-therapy, using Strategies 5 (Write Horror Stories—I wrote about my irrational fear of fire), 6 (Write Flash Fiction Stories—I put issues that bothered me on paper, such as racism and hypocrisy, although the final story is more than flash-length), 9 (Fictionalise Your Villain—he makes a brief appearance) and 11 (Write Letters To Your Younger Self—the letters served as raw material and inspiration). The final story has autobiographical elements, but is set in a different country and period, with different characters and several events combined into a single one, so nobody will recognise its origins. Factually, it is not a true story, but it has emotional truth.

Writing this took courage, but it was worth it. As soon as I'd finished the project, two remarkable things happened. My phobia of fire disappeared, and the story became a big success. It is my best-known work of fiction, has been praised by literary critics and won awards.

Supper was bangers and mash with mushy peas. Mum had promised me the glossy calendar photo for November—lambs frolicking around Camber Castle—but only if I ate up every meal this month. I disliked greasy bangers, I despised mash, and I hated mushy peas, but I wanted that picture, and it was only the ninth. Half-listening to my parents' grown-up talk about the need for a new church, I stirred the peas into the mash. Instead of becoming more appetising, the meal now looked like a vomit puddle around dog turds.

Pa's knife sliced a banger; fat spurted. His face shone with enjoyment. My brother Darren stuffed his mouth with mushy peas and smiled as if he liked the taste, which I knew he didn't. I wondered if Mum had promised him the picture, too.

Mum patted her freshly permed hair. "It's almost night." She stood up to pull the kitchen curtains against the approaching darkness, the way she always did during supper. This time she paused. "There's a lot of smoke. It looks like something's burning down by the old harbour. It glows. Holy Mother of Jesus, something's burning proper. It could be the Eversons' shop."

Standing on my toes, I peered out of the window. My breath fogged the cold glass. With the sleeve of my jumper, I wiped a patch clear, saw dark smoke spiralling toward the empty sky. A light glowed a half-mile from our house, like an orange-coloured glimpse of hell.

Pa put his fork down. "I'll go down the road and watch."

"Is it wise to get involved with this?" Uncertainty quavered in Mum's voice.

"I'm not involved." He stood up and took his grey hat and winter coat from the clothes hook on the door.

"Can I come?" Darren asked through a mouth full of blackened sauerkraut. "I've finished my supper."

Pa was already tying a grey shawl around his neck. "Yes, you can come, son." He paused, pointing his chin at me. "I'll take the girl, too."

Frightened by what I'd seen out of the window, I tried to protest. "I don't want to go. Please..."

An angry glance from Pa shut me up. His hard hand pulled me away from the table. "You'll come."

Within moments, Mum had bundled me into my anorak, a thick knitted shawl and a woollen hat. "Stay with Pa, don't catch a cold, and don't talk to anyone."

Darren grabbed his Superman jacket and cap and ran down the stairs, and I followed. At least I had escaped from the mushy peas.

Pa forced me into the black metal seat on the bar of his bicycle, so that I was locked between his body, his arms and the handlebar. At seven, I was really too old to travel in the child seat, but he seemed to like holding me captive, and I did not dare suggest I ride behind him on the luggage rack. Darren followed on his own bike.

A few minutes later, we reached the blaze, and faced it from the safety of the pavement opposite. My heartbeat roared in my ears like a locomotive. The fire was real in its frightful intensity. Thick smoke oozed through the roof and curled into grey spark-loaded columns. Hot stink wafted in our faces.

"Smells like we're burning garbage," said a woman with silver spectacles and wrinkly skin. Others laughed; their laughter sounded eerie against the whine from the fire.

Many people had come to watch the house burn. Onlookers stood in small clusters, their hands in their pockets, their faces muffled with shawls.

My mouth was dry and tense; cold prickled on my skin, and I put my hand into my father's coat pocket to hold his hand. "I want to go home, Pa. Please."

"Watch." He grabbed my shoulders and turned me towards the fire. "Watch and learn. Learn about what happens to garbage."

I tried hard not to look, but the glow drew and held me. I knew the house: The shop on the ground floor sold magazines, lottery tickets, ice cream, my favourite Werther's toffee sweets and Mum's cans of mushy peas. Above the shop was a flat, and above that, an attic under a gabled roof.

The façade looked thin and vulnerable. The upper windows contained dark emptiness, and the bow windows of the shop screamed with orange heat. Everything looked black against this orange. The house reminded me of the lanterns we'd been making at school, black cardboard with rectangular cut-outs, with brightly coloured translucent paper behind.

I didn't mind the rows of mushy peas cans burning, but I regretted the Werther's toffee and the ice cream chest.

"Are they in there?" a young woman asked in a thin voice. She carried a small white dog in her arms and stroked it incessantly. She tilted her head at my father. "The Eversons and the Arabs aren't still in there, are they?"

"I've only just arrived. I know nothing."

"If they were at home, they'd have come out by now, wouldn't they?"

When he gave no reply, she turned to the tall bespectacled woman. "The fire fighters are taking their time, aren't they?" She stepped from one foot to the other, either nervous or cold. "They've been notified, haven't they?"

"Yes," the other woman said.

"Well, they're volunteers, I suppose they can't be expected..."

"No."

"Still, why..."

The sea breeze whipped the flames into further frenzy. In the distance, seagulls screeched.

"I don't know anything, so don't ask." The older woman turned away. The younger one stopped talking, and pressed her face into her dog's coat.

Not everyone was quiet, though. Darren had met up with other boys from his class. They hurled stones at the windows of the upper stories, smashing the panes the fire hadn't reached yet, chanting something about cleaning up the town. Their teacher stood by, and I expected him to call the boys to order, but held his hands folded behind his back and watched.

Within moments, the sash windows of the upstairs flat lit up at once like a garland of festive lights. Glass crackled and tinkled, a beautiful chiming sound, dotted with poufs and bangs. The smoke grew darker and thicker, turning dirty brown and charcoal black. Plaster blistered and peeled off the wall. Embers flew.

Wind blasted from the site and threw furious heat at us. My face felt like a roasting sausage, but when I averted it, the icy night air made my hair stand up.

Sirens howled, the dog yapped, and people made room on the pavement for a shiny police car. Two uniformed policemen jumped out and shooed people back from the site, including the chanting boys. Then they stood, inactive, hypnotised like the rest of us.

Now smoke seeped from the small attic window, then it lit up as if someone had switched on a hundred lights behind a red curtain. A collective "Aah," rose from the crowd. A couple of people started to clap, but stopped when a policeman threw them a stern look.

I wasn't sure what it all meant. I couldn't believe that people were trapped inside this boiling heat. I scanned the crowd for the woman with the white dog, but she had disappeared, so I asked the woman with the spectacles. "Are there people in the fire? Are they burning?"

"Of course not, dearie," she soothed. "The Eversons are away on holiday. They had a sign in the window, 'Closed until Monday 11th'. And even if there was someone in there, they wouldn't feel a thing. The smoke would get them first. So don't you fret." She fished in her coat pocket. "Here, have a sweet, dearie." I hesitated, because my parents warned me not to take sweets from strangers, but Pa had laughed with this woman, so maybe she wasn't a stranger, and it was a Werther's toffee.

"Come on, take it."

Fearing to offend by refusing, I croaked a thank-you from my dry throat and took the sweet, but put it into my pocket.

Now a red fire engine pulled up with blue flaring lights. Dogs and sirens howled. While the fire fighters opened the hydrant and connected their thick limp hose, the burning house roared like an angry animal. The night sky now appeared deep blue, cool and clean.

I heard one fireman question a group of men. "Anyone still in there?"

"Don't think so. The Eversons own the shop and live in the flat above; they're away on holiday."

"There won't be much left of their shop and their flat when they come back."

"They're insured."

In the meantime, two fire fighters with helmets had rammed the door and gone in, but came out within moments, signalling with large arm gestures.

The fireman standing near us translated. "The staircase has collapsed. Nothing we can do."

Flames leaped high in the air, glowing orange and yellow, red and lilac, and it was the most beautiful and most horrible sight I had ever beheld. In the midst of the tumult, I heard screams from the fire.

Around me, people mumbled and shuffled their feet.

"It's the wood," someone said. "The fire has reached the ceiling beams." Another voice replied, "That's right. Old wood always sounds like that when it burns."

A fat dog howled and strained at its lead. But the people just stood, spellbound by the spectacle. The rumble and roar of the blaze absorbed any further cries. Huge billows of smoke and flame erupted when the roof burnt through, and beams and timber collapsed with a crash.

A few moments later, the fire quietened, showing what was left of the building. The floor between the ground floor and the first storey still held. Above it, all was gone, apart from a few sagging fragments of walls, and the timbers on each corner which flamed like giant altar candles.

"That house is lost for good," the fireman said. "All we can do now is stop the fire from spreading."

The acid sting of wet ash got into my nose and into my throat where it scratched and tasted bitter. As best I could, I shielded my face with the knitted shawl. Dancing ashes showered us like confetti from a carnival float.

As the fire withdrew further, the darkness grew silent and cold.

"Time to go home," Pa said to nobody in particular. "The children are getting restless."

By the time we got home, I was shivering. Although I needed to ask many questions, Mum packed me into bed and told me to be quiet and sleep.

All night images of fire plagued me, and I feared I would burn. The bitter flavours of smoke and fear clogged my throat, and I heard the sounds of crackling fire. My heart hammered and my body was bathed in cold sweat. Many times I touched the floor to check it for heat, afraid that the storey below was burning. Any moment smoke and flames might burst through and engulf me in hell fire.

In the morning, I was still upset. My hair stank of nasty smoke, and my head burnt from the uneasy night.

Mum put her hand on my forehead while we sat at breakfast. "The girl has a fever. You shouldn't have taken her out in the cold."

"You've been too soft with the children. They have to become tougher." He lit a cigarette and puffed. Normally, he didn't smoke at breakfast. The smoke curled and found its way into my nostrils.

While the others had bread with butter and blackberry jam, Mum served up bangers, mash and mushy peas. In our family, sickness was no excuse for wasting food. I recoiled at the vomit-like stuff, no less repulsive after microwaving than it had been before. Mum sniffed, but not at the food. "Holy Mother, you stink. All three of you. The smoke is in your hair."

I sliced a banger with my knife, and watched the grease run and curl around the peas-mash heap. Darren spread butter and thick blackberry jam on his bread. I glanced at the picture of the jolly lambs and decided it wasn't worth it. If Pa left for work soon, I might get away without forcing the horrid stuff down. Mum sometimes waived punishments.

The letterbox rattled, and a plop told us that the newspaper had arrived. Mum fetched it. She moved the bread-bowl to the side and spread the paper out on the kitchen table, opening it on the first page of local news.

I read the headline, one bold word after the other. "*Family Perish in Fire—Hoax Call Leads to Destruction of Shop and Homes.*"

Perish meant something like 'die'. But surely nobody had died. We'd been there, and everyone had said that the Eversons were away on holiday.

A large photo showed a smouldering ruin, a smaller one depicted fire fighters directing a blast from a hose.

Darren grabbed the paper and read aloud. "Three members of the Maqsoum family died in the fire. They were..." He mumbled the names and ages of the victims.

So people had died. They had burnt like the martyrs in the most frightening stories of *The Children's Book of Saints.* But it couldn't be true. The saints had died in faraway countries a long, long time ago, not at the end of our road last night.

The report said that the local fire fighters had been called to a non-existent fire, which made them late to arrive at the site. It described how the charred remains had been found. The mother had cowered under a table while the father and the eight-year-old twin daughters had squeezed into a corner. The man was shielding the children's bodies with his own, apparently trying to hold off the flames from them until the last possible moment.

Nausea squeezed my throat again. These people had been awake and conscious. They hadn't passed out in the smoke, as the woman with the spectacles had tried to make me believe. With a pang of guilt I remembered the Werther's toffee I had accepted from her, and resolved to smuggle it into the rubbish bin later when nobody was looking.

I realised that the Arabs had seen the flames coming, looked into the deadly orange, smelled that bitter, acid smoke. Perhaps they'd found the exit blocked, but kept hoping that someone would get them out, if only they could retreat from the fire until help arrived. They'd withdrawn, shrunk into the corner, pursued by death. Even as the flames gnawed at them, as smoke clogged their nostrils and bit their throats, even as the flames started to devour their flesh, they continued to hope, even as the father sacrificed himself to gain a few more seconds for his girls... And then they screamed. I had heard those screams of pain and despair and death.

"They suffered," Mum said. "Holy Mother of Jesus, they must have suffered. I thought they'd go without pain, from the smoke. It doesn't seem right. Even for Arabs, this can't be right."

Pa shifted uncomfortably on the corner seat. I thought he would say something to praise the Arab father's courage. Instead, he lit another cigarette and said, "I'll be off in a moment."

Mum recovered and turned her attention to us. "Never play with matches," she lectured. "I've always told you so. Now you know what comes from being careless with fire."

"They were only Arabs," Darren said with the superiority of a twelve-year-old. "Dirty people. It was a dirty flat they lived in, full of clutter. Arabs live like that. I mean, just think of it. Four people in a one-bedroom flat. Decent people wouldn't live like that."

Although I didn't follow his reasoning, I accepted that the deaths had been at least partly the Arabs' fault, because of the way they lived, and because they had probably been careless with matches. I clutched my mug of hot milk.

"Why didn't they get out?" Mum wondered aloud. "They must have heard the fire, smelled something. They can't have been asleep at that time."

"Don't get involved." Pa took his coat and left.

Because of my fever, Mum made me stay in bed all day and brought me chamomile tea and hot water bottles. I sweated in the heat.

I could almost feel the hot breath of fire on my arms, and closed my eyes against the pain. In my mind, I crowded in the corner with the Arab family. We were trying to shield one another from the inevitable fire, the fear, the stinging leaps, the bites of the flames.

I thought of my own family. Strangely, I couldn't imagine Pa shielding us. I felt a yearning for the kind of love this Arab father had for his daughters.

In the evening, Mum made me sit at the kitchen table, either because she thought my fever had gone, or because she didn't want to annoy Pa. She plunked the plate of old food before me, not even bothering to reheat it in the microwave.

I was saved when a visitor came: the old woman with the silver spectacles. Mum patted her hair as if to check that the waves were still in place, and swiftly removed the plate with the disgusting food. Instead, she gave me and the woman fresh plates and we ate bread and mustard like the others. Of course talk turned to the fire again.

"Shame about the shop," the woman said. "I know Everson wants to move to more central premises where he can have a tea room, but it's still a huge loss."

Pa smiled. "They have insurance."

I didn't understand this grown-up talk, but had a vague idea that insurance prevented families from getting burnt. "Do we have insurance?" I asked.

"We don't need it. We don't have Arabs living in our house."

The mention of the Arabs made me cry.

"The girl's upset," the woman said. "It's been too much for her. She's so young. How old are you, dearie?"

"Seven," I managed between sobs. Then I asked the question I had wanted to ask all day. "Are they saints now? Have they gone to heaven?"

"No, dearie, they're Arabs. Arabs don't go to heaven."

I cried more. I wanted them to go to heaven.

Mum tried to console me. "Maybe there's something like a lower heaven where Arabs can go. Other heathens as well, if they've been good." She patted my hand. "Remember when your cat died? Maybe there's a heaven for cats and Arabs and other animals."

Darren giggled, and Pa snorted. "There's nothing in the Bible about that."

For a moment, all was quiet. Mum's mouth twitched like she might cry, too.

The visitor spoke into the silence. "If Everson doesn't rebuild, the site would suit our new church."

"We could use a new church." Relief sang in Mum's voice. "Something good is coming out of this after all." She folded her hands in her lap and smiled.

Pa and the neighbour smiled, too, because everything was good and right.

EXCERPT: WRITING DEEP POINT OF VIEW

INTRODUCTION

Do you want to give the readers such a vivid experience that they feel the events of the story are real and they're right there? Do you want them to forget their own world and worries, and live in the main character's head and heart?

The magic wand for achieving this is Deep Point of View.

Deep Point of View is a recent development. Victorian authors didn't know its power. They wrote stories from a god-like perspective, knowing everything, seeing into everyone's mind and soul. 20th century writers discovered that when they let the reader into just one person's head, stories became more exciting and real.

If we take this one step further, and delve so deeply into one person's mind that the reader's awareness merges with that character's, we have Deep Point of View.

Readers love it, because it gives them the thrill of becoming a different person. The reader doesn't just read a story about a gladiator in the arena, an heiress in a Scottish castle, an explorer in the jungle, a courtesan in Renaissance Venice—she becomes that gladiator, heiress, explorer, courtesan.

Deep Point of View hooks readers from the start. After perusing the sample, he'll click 'buy now' because he simply must read on, and when he's reached the last page, he's grown addicted to the character, doesn't want the story to end, and buys the next book in the series at once.

A reader who has been in the grip of Deep Point of View may find other books dull and shallow. Who wants to read about a pirate, when you can be a pirate yourself? Immersed in Deep PoV, the reader enjoys the full thrills of the adventure from the safety of her armchair.

In this book, I'll reveal the powerful techniques employed by bestselling authors, and I'll show you how to apply them to rivet your readers. I'll start with the basics of Point of View—if you're already familiar with the concept, you can treat them as a refresher—and then guide you to advanced strategies for taking your reader deep.

This is not a beginners' book. It assumes that you have mastered the basics of the writer's craft and know how to create compelling fictional characters. If you like, you can use this book as a self-study class, approaching each chapter as a lesson and completing the assignments at the end of each session.

To avoid clunky constructions like 'he or she did this to him or her' I use sometimes 'he' and sometimes 'she'. With the exception of Chapter 6, everything I write applies to either gender. I use British English, so my grammar, punctuation, spellings and word choices may differ from what you're used to in American.

Now let's explore how you can lead your readers deep into your story.

Rayne Hall

CHAPTER 1: FRESH PERSPECTIVES

Instead of explaining Point of View, I'll let you experience it. Let's do a quick practical exercise.

Wherever you are right now, look out of the window (or step out into the open, or do whatever comes closest). If possible, open the window and stick your head out. What do you notice?

Return to your desk or notebook, and jot down two sentences about your spontaneous observations.

You can jot down anything—the cars rushing by, the rain-heavy clouds drawing up on the horizon, the scent of lilacs, the wasps buzzing around the dumpster, the aeroplane scratching the sky, the empty beer cans in the gutter, the rain-glistening road, whatever.

Don't bother writing beautiful prose—only the content matters. And only two sentences.

When you've done this—but not before—read on.

*

*

*

Have you written two sentences about what you observed outside the window? Good. Now we'll have fun.

Imagine that you're a different person. Pick one of these:

1. A 19-year-old female student, art major, currently planning to create a series of paintings of townscapes, keenly aware of colours and shapes.

2. A professional musician with sharp ears and a keen sense of rhythm.

3. An eighty-year-old man with painful arthritic knees which get worse in cold weather. He's visiting his daughter and disapproves of the place where she's living these days.

4. A retired health and safety inspector.

5. An architect whose hobby is local history.

6. A hobby gardener with a keen sense of smell.

7. A security consultant assessing the place where a foreign royal princess is going to walk among the people next week.

Once again, stick your head out of the window. What do you notice this time? Return to your desk and jot down two sentences.

I bet the observations are very different! Each time, you saw, heard and smelled the same place—but the first time you experienced it as yourself (from your Point of View) and the second time, as a fictional character (from that character's PoV).

You may want to repeat this exercise with another character from the list, to deepen your insight and practise the skill. If you're an eager learner, do all seven. This will give you a powerful understanding of how PoV works.

Now let's take it one step further: Imagine you're the main character from the story you're currently writing (or have recently finished). How would he experience this place? What would he notice above all else? Again, write two sentences.

Now you've experienced the power of PoV, this is how you will write all your fiction.

ASSIGNMENT

Repeat this exercise in a different place—perhaps when you have time to kill during a train journey or in the dentist's waiting room.

Printed in Poland
by Amazon Fulfillment
Poland Sp. z o.o., Wrocław

72306838R00054